CHAMPIONSHIP
SPORTS
PSYCHOLOGY

by
Dr. Keith Bell

Library of Congress Cataloging-in-Publication Data

Bell, Keith F.
  [Championship thinking]
  Championship sports psychology / by Keith Bell.
      p.   cm.
  Reprint. Originally published as: Championship
  thinking. Englewood Cliffs, N.J.: Prentice-Hall,
  c1983
  Includes bibliographical references (p.)
  ISBN 0-945609-04-3: $21.95
  1. Sports—Psychological aspects. 2. Motivation
  (Psychology) I. Title.
GV706.4.B559   1990
796'.01—dc20   *89-49136*
                                                       CIP

Cover design by **Keith Bell** & **Sandy Neilson-Bell**.
Olympic Gold Medals provided by
Sandy Neilson-Bell.

Printed in the United States of America.

10 9 8 7 6 5 4 3 2

This book is available at a special discount
when ordered in bulk quantities.

Published and distributed by:
            KEEL PUBLICATIONS
            P.O. Box 160155
            Austin, Texas 78716
            (512) 327-1280

For Sandy, Kirsten, Keena, Bridger and Cooper,
who fill my world with joy, vitality and
immeasurable beauty.

CONTENTS

PREFACE

Winning performances are not only the goal but the joy of sports. Those magic moments when you put it all together and are "hot," "in the zone," "playing out of your head," or "in the groove" produce unusually good results, while providing vivifying and elating experiences.

Peak performances are truly remarkable. They can be tremendously exciting while at the same time enormously peaceful. Perception may seem to be altered. You may have a heightened sensitivity. And you may perceive things more fully and with extraordinary clarity.

Time may seem to slow down or somehow seem irrelevant. Swimmers and runners report feeling as if they were moving in slow motion as they recorded their fastest performances. Runner Steve Williams says that when a 100 is done right, "ten seconds seem like sixty."[1] Former Los Angeles Ram quarterback Pat Haden has reported moments when "the three-and-a-half seconds between the snap from center and the time you release the ball seem like a month."[2] He says, "It's the most exhilarating feeling you could ever imagine: very pure, simple."[3]

Golfers report "knowing" the ball is going in the cup and "seeing" the exact line the ball will follow. Baseball players report seeing the ball coming in so big that they can almost count the stitches. Tennis champ Rod Laver suggests that

> You can go out on court some days and feel so sharp and so alert that the ball comes over the net looking as big as a soccer ball, and you think to yourself there's no way I can make a mistake.[4]

These moments are totally engaging and absorbing. They combine with the thrill of victory to produce an athlete's ultimate high. But are they replicable?

When you are "on your game," playing at your best, it seems so natural and so easy. You feel completely in control. You wonder how you could ever perform at lower levels. Yet these moments fade away as easily as they come. Then you wonder if you can ever match these levels of performance again. You wait. And you hope that you will get it back.

But you do not have to be content with waiting—you can do something about it. You can learn psychological skills that can be employed to get you performing at peak levels more consistently. And with practice these skills will plug in automatically, allowing you to let loose, get with the flow, and enjoy your winning performances.

Many books on sports psychology make suggestions that are difficult to get a handle on. Some even seem somewhat mystical; they can leave you uncertain as to what to do or how to do it.

In this book, I have endeavored to provide you with a practical guide to winning performances. Peak athletic performances are too exciting, rewarding, and intrinsically pleasurable to grope after.

In Part II, I have identified the psychological challenges facing you as an athlete and provided you with practical suggestions for meeting them. In Part I, I have presented the psychological tools you will need to meet these challenges.

I hope you will eagerly devour this book. If you want, however, to get the most out of what sports psychology has to offer, a cursory reading will not suffice. You need to put the information to work. Carefully, go over each section, understand the issues, mold the tools to fit your particular situation, sharpen the skills you acquire, and *practice* their application. As with most anything, the more you put into understanding, rehearsing, and applying **Championship Sports Psychology,** the greater the returns.

If you are already meeting some of the psychological challenges of sports successfully, it makes little sense to work on those particular areas. Don't make good, free-flowing habits into conscious acts. On the other hand, everyone has areas that are ripe for improvement. Those areas warrant detailed attention and concerted effort.

Although I regularly work with athletes and teams representing every sport and have cited examples from many different sports, I have frequently referred to examples from competitive swimming to illustrate points. Swimming is what I know best. I have coached NCAA, AIAW, and club swimming teams. I began swimming competitively at the age of eight, swam throughout college, and, more than 25 years later, am still training hard and actively competing in masters swimming competitions. This complete immersion (pardon the pun) in the world of swimming provides a frame of reference important for specifying the subtle psychological challenges inherent in training and competition and ways for dealing with them. Your vantage point should allow you specific application to your sport.

For that matter, the book is written for athletes but really explores applications of principles and techniques from human performance psychology. (In this case, to the world of sports.) It is my hope that athletes and nonathletes alike will find it of interest—and that you will use my ideas and suggestions to enhance the quality of your life in other, nonathletic fields of endeavor as well.

In my swimming, I am continuously applying, practicing, and trying out psychological techniques in training and in competition. It has worked for me. I am training harder, performing better, and enjoying it more than ever before—largely due to improved psychological strategies. You can, too!

Naturally, there are no guarantees in the world of sports. Adequate or even superlative mental preparation will not necessarily enable you to forge a pro career, make the Olympic team, or even record a personal best. There are too many other factors involved, not the least of which is physical preparation. Nor can the gifts of heredity be ignored.

There is no question, however, that psychological considerations are integral factors in determining how well you perform at sports. Arnold Palmer has said, "Ninety percent of golf is played from the shoulders up." Maury Wills has called baseball "all mental." The quotations reflecting this idea go on ad infinitum. The percentages cited are arbitrary, but the sentiment is well taken.

Recent advances in physical training, stemming from studies of exercise physiology, kinesiology, biomechanics, and the strategies and philosophies of sports have led to a greater intensity and uniformity of training. Subsequently, competitions have become more tightly contested at increasingly higher levels of performance. Margins of victory often are not only inches and seconds, but millimeters and thousandths of seconds. As a result, psychological factors have become even more important in defining the winner. Brian Gottfried says that in professional tennis "everyone has the strokes. The difference in the players is all mental."[5] Serge Vaitsekhovsky, the head coach for the Soviet national swimming team, has gone so far as to declare that "victory is not a question of training. Everyone trains. It is a question of psychology."[6] Settle that question by using this book as a guide to building the psychological foundations of championship performances.

PART ONE
THE TOOLS

1
CHAMPIONSHIP THINKING

What we think while playing . . . is probably the single most important part of any player's game.[1]

GARY PLAYER

By nature, we are cognitive animals. We are constantly talking to ourselves and appraising what is going on around us. We make attributions and interpretations of our world. We filter our experience through our biases, assumptions, and beliefs and behave accordingly. We not only react to what we perceive in our environment, we interact with it, actively affecting it. For these reasons, our cognition (thoughts and images) play an important role in determining level of performance. What you do, when you do it, how you feel before, during, and after your performances, and how well you perform and will perform again are largely determined by your thoughts.

Yet many athletes report that superior performances seem to be accompanied by less conscious effort. Peak performances seem to find these athletes so completely involved in what they are doing that they have no thoughts of doing it correctly, no thoughts of failure, and no thoughts of fatigue.

Some authors have suggested that quieting your thoughts can lead to peak performance. The tennis coach Timothy Gallwey asserts that "athletes in most sports . . . know that their peak performance never comes when they're thinking about it."[2] He tells you to get "the unconscious or automatic functions . . . working without interference from thoughts."[3] Maxwell Maltz, the plastic surgeon and author of *Psycho-Cybernetics* recommends visualizing your goals and letting your "automatic goal-seeking servo-mechanism" take over.[4] In fact, frequently it appears that relaxed, effortless concentration and automatic performance seem not only to accompany (or be an integral part of) outstanding performances, but to constitute an overwhelmingly enjoyable experience in itself.

We cannot, however, neglect the role of our conscious cognitive activity in determining how well we perform. First and foremost, despite the benefits of getting so totally absorbed in the game that you just "let it happen," the fact remains that you will think. You may strive for those brief, concentrated moments of performance that seem free of thought, but most of the time your performances will be replete with thinking.

You Will Think

Consider golf or tennis. When you are really "on your game" you do not consciously seem to think much. In fact, the more you think about what you are doing *while you are doing it*, the less "in the groove" you are. In these two sports, the actual task (hitting the ball) requires much less than a second to perform. Focused attention on these split-second acts does not allow for the interference of thoughts. There is not time to think about what you are doing and still do it well. Yet in tennis, even when you are in the flow, you think between points, if not between shots. Bjorn Borg even has described tournament tennis as "four hours of thinking, thinking, on every point."[5] In golf, there is a tremendous amount of time between shots, during which, inevitably, you think. In fact, Gary Player says golf is "made for psychology" because of "all those lonely walks between shots when you have to think about what to do instead of just reacting."[6]

In other sports, where responding is more sustained, thoughts are prevalent during performance. In competitive swimming, for example, as of this writing, no one has swum even the shortest race in less than 19 seconds. During that length of time a swimmer will experience at least a few fleeting thoughts. Longer races are occasion for much more thought. Likewise, it is inconceivable for anyone to run an entire marathon without thinking.

Even if you could quiet your thoughts for an entire event, which you cannot, what about practices? You could not go through hours and hours of practice daily without thinking. Nor would you want to. Properly directed thinking helps you to challenge successfully the demands of your sport, the efforts of your opponents, and your human limitations.

To Think or Not to Think Is Not the Question: Rather, It Is What, When, and How to Think

In your quest for superlative performances, whether or not to think does not seem to be a relevant question. Thoughts and images are integral to human functioning. Sports provide no exception.

The more salient issue seems to be what, when, and how to think. It is not thinking itself that impedes superlative performance. The human capacity to think is your greatest aid to performances. It is inappropriate or misguided thinking that often leads to substandard performance. What you think about prior to, accompanying, and following your performance, the timing of your thoughts, and the way you think (the thought process) make the critical difference in determining what you do, how well you do it, and how you feel. Fortunately, although much of this cognitive activity appears to occur spontaneously, you can learn to control your thoughts with intentional thinking. Championship thinking is within your grasp.

LEARN TO LISTEN TO YOUR THOUGHTS

On occasion, we are acutely aware of actively talking to ourselves. Much of our thinking, however, seems to go unnoticed unless we focus in on it intentionally. No matter that our thoughts exert a tremendous influence on us; we often pay little attention to them. We seem either to be unaware of much of this thought, or else it does not occur to us that our thoughts may be playing an important role in determining how well we do.

Part of our inattention to thought may stem from its automatic nature. Our thoughts seem to occur automatically and involuntarily. Most often, we make no attempt to initiate thought. It just happens. Yet when directed to attend to our thoughts, most of us become increasingly aware of them.

The first step to gaining control of your thoughts is increased awareness. You want to identify and know what kind of thinking helps, what thoughts hurt, and what your usual thought patterns are. If you are aware of what you are saying to yourself that primes you for good performance, guides you through it, and helps you to successfully cope with obstacles along the way, then you have cognitive tools at your disposal that you can use to enhance performance. On the other hand, identifying what you say or fail to say to yourself in those instances when performance or enjoyment falls short does not, in itself, provide a means for improvement. But it does let you know what you are up against. Then you can devise, practice, and apply strategies for improvement.

There are a number of ways you can learn how certain thoughts affect your performance. The most common, though not necessarily the most productive way, is through introspection. By reflecting upon previous experience you can often identify thoughts that significantly aided or deterred good performance. In doing so, try to draw from a wide range of experiences, collecting as much data as you can. Here, as in all of these information-gathering techniques, be sure to include training circumstances. Do not limit yourself to major competitions. Rather focus on those situations in which you performed particularly well despite major obstacles, or especially poorly in practice or in competition. These will provide the most useful information.

A second method is to imagine yourself in a variety of situations related to training and competition in your sport and observe your thoughts as you imaginally participate. Some athletes find it helpful to "run a movie through their head" of a recent performance (practice or competition), noting their cognitive activity. This is an excellent method. You should take care to imagine the "movie" as if you were in it, actively participating from the viewpoint of your "self," rather than to view yourself participating. Again, use this technique to concentrate on significant events.

A third method is to reconstruct the thoughts, images, and feelings you experienced during a previous performance while viewing a videotape or motion picture. Of course, the sooner after your performance you can view the film, the more accurate your reconstruction is likely to be.

Most commonly, videotape is used to capture the action of competition or training in order to analyze strategy and mechanics. For our purposes here, it is in addition particularly important to get the moments preceding performance and the pauses in action on tape. Thus, tape of a runner sitting while waiting to be called to the blocks, a diver on the board preparing to approach his dive, a gymnast putting powder on her hands, a tennis player between games and between shots, a golfer walking to her lie, and so forth, can provide the stimulus for re-creation of thinking that was critical to the level of performance.

With all of the above methods there exists the danger of distortion. Nevertheless, most athletes have substantial success in acquiring useful information. The most accurate way of gathering this information comes from monitoring your thoughts during the actual performance. By listening to yourself with a "third ear," you can directly observe your cognitive activity while it occurs, rather than having to reconstruct it.

This method, although the most accurate, is not without disadvantages. It is likely that the very act of observing your thoughts as you perform will alter the quality and nature of both the internal behavior you are observing and your overt performance. You risk interrupting the automaticity of response that characterizes peak performance. For this reason direct observation of your thoughts best takes place during practice and minor competitions. This is not the method of choice during major competitions. It is best to handle those situations with the other previously mentioned techniques.

As you listen to your thoughts look for common themes or links running through your thoughts. Of particular interest are thoughts associated with noticeably desirable (or undesirable) performances.

These are the ones you want to repeat (or change). It is best to keep a written record of your findings. Formal observation of this sort will facilitate working out a structured program for improvement. More casual observation and haphazard recording leave too much to chance.

As you monitor and record your thoughts you will notice that they take a variety of forms. Your thoughts may be very explicit verbalizations or self-statements. Often, however, they tend to appear in a kind of shorthand fashion consisting of unfinished sentences, rhetorical questions, or cue words that have some special meanings to you. They may take a pictoral form, consisting of images instead of words. Or in some cases you may merely be aware of a certain feeling (nervousness, for example) rather than a distinct image or verbalization. In any case, you will find that these cognitions convey specific and discrete messages— no matter what their form or how idiosyncratic.

Make these messages explicit. Write specific messages represented by cue words. Put words to the images and feelings, giving them a verbal form. And make explicit the hidden or implicit messages suggested by the observed thoughts, recording them in writing. For example, the rhetorical question "What if I don't win?" often means something like "I probably won't win. And when I fail to win, it will be terrible." Similarly, a somewhat vague feeling of apprehension might reflect a pessimistic prediction of the likely outcome or, in a strength or endurance event, a message suggesting that "the pain will be intense and I won't be able to stand it."

It is not as important to alter the form of the thoughts that are aiding superlative performances. Making these explicit, however, may aid in your ability to use them in a wider variety of situations, increasing the consistency of your performances. It is important, however, that you explicitly identify the cognitions associated with poor performances, verbalizing them and ferreting out any implicit messages. This crystallization will aid you in generating strategies for improvement.

Be sure to include situations where something you failed to say to yourself led to substandard performances. Naturally, it will be difficult to remember, recreate, or observe what you did *not* think. Those times when you reproached yourself for not thinking or admonished yourself to "think" were likely circumstances where you missed the opportunity to improve your performance by intentionally producing self-instructional statements.

Self-monitoring is an important first step in controlling your thoughts. It often can provide some benefit even without further intentional action. Deficient self-monitoring of thought and impulse is often seen in the lack of self-control that characterizes giving in to the pain, fatigue, boredom, or temptations that interfere with diligent training or effortful performance. The information gained through observing your thoughts also may be subtly applied, improving performance in the absence of any apparent effort. For the most part, however, it is merely one stage in the quest for psychological advantage.

Some caution is well advised. As mentioned above, monitoring your thoughts can interfere with the "flow" of good performances. As a result, observation of the thoughts associated with good performance should be limited to a search for thoughts that can be applied intentionally to further improvement under similar circumstances.

Monitoring thoughts accompanying poor performances is only useful if it sets the occasion for further action. Without corrective action, overattention to your negative thoughts often leads to self-consciousness and self-criticism, even further debilitating already poor performances.

Listen to your thinking. But use the monitoring of your thoughts as the initial step toward developing and utilizing thinking habits that will aid consistency and excellence of performance.

Throughout this book I will make suggestions about what kinds of thinking aid performance and will provide examples. But don't limit yourself to these ideas and those that you get from examining your own experience. Ask coaches and other successful athletes what they have noticed about their thinking and how it has corresponded with their performance. And be creative. Generate new ideas. A vast repertoire of performance-enhancing cognitions is desirable.

Don't create or industriously gather a large list of negative self-statements. You have no use for these. The only negative self-talk of interest is the thoughts that frequently or occasionally interfere with your performance. You will want to manage these.

On the other hand, well-timed, specific, task-relevant self-statements can aid and support your efforts to achieve consistent excellence of performance. Let's look at some specific kinds of thinking you can utilize toward these ends.

SELF-INSTRUCTIONAL METHODS

"Keep your eye on the ball."
"Keep your head down."
"Follow through."
"Pick it up."
"Stretch."
"Relax."
"Stay with it."
"Arms up."
"Keep your elbows up."
"Don't worry about the other guy—swim your own race."
"Think."

Instructions refer to statements describing the relationship between events. They describe, direct, and activate performance. Instructions tell you what to do, when to do it, and how to do it. They direct your attention and they guide your responses.

Instruction is one of the most powerful and effective means of directing and initiating behavior. Just think how much of what you do is controlled by interpersonal instructions or self-instructional statements.

Self-instructions occur naturally. The sequence of appraising and interpreting a situation, debating options, and making decisions leads logically to self-instructions. You assess the situation confronting you (with an eye toward your goals) and then direct your behavior with explicit verbal messages. Even when a coach or someone else makes the decisions for you, you internalize their directions, blending their instructions with your self-instructions.

While your actions are constantly mediated by self-instructions, it is likely that you are aware of going around talking to yourself, telling yourself what to do. Rather, you seem to respond automatically. But by intentionally instructing yourself in situations where your automatic reactions are not likely to produce the best goal-directed behavior, you can improve your performance.

Self-instructions are particularly effective in learning a new skill, changing habits, preparing for performance, initiating action, sustaining effort, and coping with obstacles to your goals.

Learning New Skills

Much of your behavior is nonreflective. You act seemingly involuntarily (almost reflexively) in response to subtle cues from the environment. This automaticity of response is lacking when you are first learning the skills of your sport. Then specific instructions elicit, direct, and guide your performance until practice yields overlearning and more habitual responding.

Those of you who drive a car may remember what it was like to learn. At first, you needed to instruct yourself during each step. You actually thought about it and told yourself to adjust the mirror, buckle your seatbelt, check to see that the car is in neutral, turn the key, step on the gas, and so on. When turning, you told yourself to switch on your turn signal, to turn hand over hand, to change lanes slowly, and the like. You might have learned to tell yourself to apply the brakes gently and gradually as if there were an egg beneath the pedal and you did not want to break it. After a while, however, the process became so well learned that this explicit self-talk was no longer necessary. Now you often seem to drive without thinking about it. Much of the time you probably do not even recall how you got from one place to another.

How explicit instructions should be depends on your level of skill. The more familiar the task, the less detailed the instructions need to be. As new behaviors become learned, your self-instructions become shortened, consisting only of cue words. Finally, the process may become totally void of all thinking. Your movements become fluid and automatic. In short, performance of completely unfamiliar tasks requires very detailed instructions, while performance of a more familiar task needs less direction, and performance of a well-learned skill is interrupted by too much instruction. In the last case, simple instructions to focus your attention on the task or to initiate action work better.

Consider learning how to serve in tennis. Even if you have never played tennis, learning can be facilitated by telling yourself to swing the racket much like you throw a ball. If you have never thrown a ball, more detailed instructions are required. If you know the basic movements and can put them together into one gross movement (the serve), you may best be able to aid learning merely by instructing yourself to observe the results and notice how it feels when the ball goes where you want it to.

This is different, however, from just letting it happen. Automatic responding requires familiarity with the mechanics of the movement, knowledge of the desired goal, and practice in execution. You need to know how to hit the ball, decide where it is supposed to go, and do it many times before you can just let it happen.

Even Timothy Gallwey, who advocates a natural learning that involves less thinking and more letting it happen, states that "instructions properly given and used can help a player to discover his groove faster than if he were left on his own." Unfortunately, when he said that, he was speaking of interpersonal instructions, not self-instructions. Gallwey devotes a major portion of The Inner Game of Tennis to "how-to-do-it" instructions on how not to give yourself "how-to-do-it" instructions. Nevertheless, Gallwey instructs his pupils to "let it happen," "to become aware of their feet," to "just let your racket contact the ball where it wants to," and so forth. It would be naïve to think that individuals do not internalize these modeled statements and actively instruct themselves in the same vein. These self-instructions aid even Gallwey's kind of outer-focused learning.

The content, form, and complexity of instructions differentially benefit learning, varying with your level of proficiency. Obviously, at any level, overly detailed, complex, or cumbersome instructions can inhibit learning and performance. But they are not necessary. You don't need to know how to wire a house to turn on a light. Nor do you need to know how to engineer a TV to turn it on and watch it. Similarly, an outfielder does not have to compute consciously where a batted ball will fall by calculating the curvature of its path (based on gravity), its direction of flight, the effects of the wind, its initial velocity and rate of deceleration, and so on in order to catch the ball. By the time he did all that, the runner would have scored. On the other hand, instructions to keep his eye on the ball, how to position himself in the field for a particular batter, which foot to move first, and/or to use both hands can aid in acquiring fielding skills.

Changing Habits

A habit is a behavior that is so well learned and practiced that it occurs almost automatically in certain situations. It is as if by practicing something enough you forge a groove into which your behavior automatically falls. Like a well-traveled path through a very thick forest, that's the route you follow.

Although habits are performed involuntarily, without much prior or accompanying thought, they are learned behaviors. You can learn to respond differently. Intentional self-instructional thought makes your behavior more conscious, interrupting performance. Such thinking "deautomatizes" the old act and paves the way for new responding.

For example, when swimming if you guide yourself through a flip turn with detailed instructions to pull with both arms, duck your head and bring your knees toward your nose, roll to the wall, push off on your side with your hands crossed, elbows straight, and head ducked down between your arms, and start your first pull with your lower arm, you might interrupt your smoothly flowing, "grooved," old way of turning. Normally, this process will temporarily disrupt performance. This, however, is precisely what you want to do. You want to gain control over an automatic act so you can make some changes. Eventually, with practice, you will build new and better habits that will pay off in the long run.

Completely altering your performance often necessitates detailed self-instructions. On the other hand, minor adjustments may require only minimal interruption with thoughts. For example, you may only need to remind yourself to step into the ball, instead of verbally directing your whole swing.

Habit change is aided by thinking about the new desired way of performing, rather than thinking about how not to do it. Thinking not to do something is like practicing doing the very thing you want to avoid. For example, try not to think about elephants. Notice that the instruction not to think about elephants directs your thoughts to elephants.

Not only does thinking about what not to do direct your attention to the very act you wish to avoid, it also fails to provide direction for the desired act. Self-instructions describing the desired behavior focus your efforts more productively. Most often the new habit is incompatible with performance in the old way. So while you are forging a new habit, you are eliminating the old without any attention to it. Thus, it makes much more sense to tell yourself to keep your elbow up, for example, than it does to tell yourself not to drop your elbow.

Too often, people try to change habits with instructions that follow the performance. Instructions are much more effective when preceding the desired act than when following performance. Thus, reminding yourself to "think about what you are doing" immediately before you do it is more helpful to changing ineffective habits than is the frequently heard admonition that "you gotta think" following a blown opportunity.

Preparing for Performance

There is no substitute for preparation. Practice of skills, rehearsal of strategy, and conditioning of the body are prerequisites for good competitive performance. But training for competition is not the only preparation. Even preparation for practice sessions and individual drills helps you get more out of your training. Given your level of skill, strength, and conditioning at any given time, you immediately perform better (in competition or training) if you have a clear idea of what you are trying to accomplish and how best to do it.

Self-instructional thinking expedites this mental preparation. By asking yourself questions about the nature of the task you face and answering those questions, you tell yourself exactly what to do or what not to do, and when and how to do it. Then when faced with the competitive or training situation, you are prepared to initiate the desired action and guide appropriate responding. Thus, Lou Piniella, who called himself a "thinking man's hitter," said, "When I go up to the plate, I have a pretty good idea of what they're going to do to me and what I'm going to try to do."[7]

Similarly, you might ask yourself questions like "How do I want to swim this race (set)?" "What would I do well to think about?" "How can I beat this guy?" or "What time(s) do I want to shoot for?" Then answer these questions in the form of cognitive planning and rehearsal. Self-instructions like the following set the stage for appropriate task execution: "Take it out loose and fast, then negative-split it" "Don't worry about the outcome—relax and think about what you are doing." "Go to his left side." "Descend the set to one minute and fifty-three seconds." "Pitch him high and away."

Initiating Action

Getting started can be no small obstacle. It often seems as if we are faced with overcoming overwhelming inertia. Of course, this is never true. As long as we are alive, we are constantly in action. In reality, the problem would be better described as redirecting action. Often this involves increasing effort. Moving from sitting in a chair doing nothing to getting up and dressing in your jogging clothes sometimes can be the biggest step in getting in an evening run. It is easy to get into a trancelike state, where it feels as though you have lost control of your body and could not move if you wanted to. Similarly, you can get locked into swimming at a particular pace, for example. The momentum and rhythm of what you are doing can make it just as hard (or harder) to pick it up as does fatigue. I don't know how many times in a long race it has taken me more than one lap following a decision to pick it up before doing so. Obviously, in those cases, I had enough strength left to do it, because eventually I did. But making that change can be very difficult. Other times I never made it, though I am reasonably certain I was physically capable.

Sometimes terminating the action is difficult. Again, so often it seems easier to continue what you are doing than to change, even when the change is obviously for the better and the act itself is within your repertoire of skills.

Following a long, arduous training session, when I am tired and weak, I can begin eating and continue shoveling food into my face beyond the point of being full. Once I start there is no stopping me. (I call this the "ravenous rages.") This is particularly easy to do if I am reading at the same time. I get lost in my reading and fail to realize I am eating until my stomach hurts (if then!) or, more likely, when my reading material runs out. Even if I am aware of what I am doing, that does not necessarily help me to stop—even though I am obviously capable of sitting still without eating or of getting up and moving from the table. Thoughts like "I'm eating too much" or "I've got to stop" accurately appraise my behavior and the value of alternative behaviors, but they do not necessarily evoke the desired action. When paired with self-instructions, however, they work tremendously well. Simple instructional statements like an emphatic "Stop!" or "Do it!" are effective means of initiating action.

Similarly, thoughts like "Pick it up" usually bring about the desired increase in pace, while those such as "Get up!" can stimulate your rising from a chair and getting ready for your run.

A simple, intentionally and emphatically thought self-instruction like "Do it!" "Go!" "Pick it up!" "Stop!" or "Cool it!" often can be the best method of initiating action. We tend to respond quickly and consistently to imperative statements. Consider how quickly you are likely to react to commands like these from a respected coach. Self-imposed directives often work just as well.

Sustaining Effort

Overcoming "inertia" sometimes can be difficult. Once you get going, however, remaining active often is easy. In fact, much of the attraction of sport lies in the inherent pleasure of physical activity. It just plain feels good to run under a pass, flow through the water, throw or hit a ball, kick a ball into a net, rip a dive—especially if you are doing it well and are in the flow. At such times, you often hate to have to stop.

Eventually fatigue sets in and activity can become strained. Coping with fatigue and pain is always a crucial task for the athlete in the power and endurance sports and can be for any athlete engaged in a conditioning program or straining for new heights of performance (see Chapter 7). But fatigue is not the only obstacle to continued activity. When that activity is at a level that requires effortful responding, the effort is not easily sustained; it must be exerted continuously and intentionally.

Self-instructions such as "Hold on to it!" "Push!" "Stay with it!" "Go!" and "Keep it up!" aid in sustaining effort. Without the attention to intentionally produced effort that self-instructions such as these direct, performance naturally tails off.

Coping With Obstacles

Like anything else we do, our athletic endeavors are replete with obstacles to a smooth ride to our goals. In many ways, it is the very challenge of overcoming obstacles that brings excitement, exhilaration, and intrigue to sports. We strive to overcome our physical, emotional, and cognitive limitations; the restrictions of our environment; and the planning, preparation, skill and effort of our opponents. The greater the struggle, the greater the satisfaction in victory. Thus, we provide handicaps. We separate competitors by sex, age, and level of skill. And we try to match opponents evenly in order to intensify the struggle. When there is no competition left, we vie for records. The longest winning streaks, the farthest throws, the fastest runs and swims, the highest scores, the best batting average—all these reflect artificial obstacles that augment the challenge of sport.

In the midst of seeking out additional obstacles, we simultaneously strive to conquer each and every one. Part of the struggle (a large part!) is psychological.

Inevitably, the cognitive skills employed to cope with obstacles include self-instructional methods. Ultimately, we are concerned with action. (Performance is the bottom line.) Self-instructions elicit, guide, direct, and sustain action. By pairing other performance-enhancing thoughts, beliefs, and perspectives with self-instructions, we put their gains into action.

For example, you might couple reminders of the importance of what you are doing with directives to increase your effort. In his world record 1976 Olympic Gold Medal 1500-meter freestyle swim, Brian Goodell reportedly kept saying to himself: "This is the Olympics; this is the final; *get going!*"[8] Similarly, when faced with the pain in the same race Brian coped with it by noticing it and telling himself what to do. He thought: "Well, here's the pain, *forget it* and go."[9]

When doubts about your ability and your likelihood of success creep in to threaten motivation and confidence, similar action can be taken. Late in the same race Brian found himself trailing, and thinking: "You're too far behind; you can't catch them." At which point he fought the doubts with self-instructions to "get out, get going . . . let go of the cookie."[10]

A major step in coping with any obstacle lies in attending to what you are doing. Yet we constantly are bombarded by all sorts of stimuli from the environment. Sorting out this information and directing our attention appropriately is a key to getting the job done. Unfortunately, some of the main obstacles to good performance come from our own thoughts.

Irrelevant self-talk is distracting. If you are replaying the last point on your internal videotape machine, you will probably lose the next one. If you are rehearsing what you are going to say to your date tonight while you are swimming a drill in practice, you are bound to lose some speed. Especially in a sport like swimming where practices can be long, challenging, and performed in a state of almost complete sensory deprivation, your thoughts are bound to wander. Task-relevant instructions keep you focused on what you are doing and leave little room for irrelevant thoughts. When you do lose it, self-instructions like "Think," "Concentrate on what you are doing," "Pull," "Charge the net," and "Keep your eye on the ball," can get you back on track.

Use Self-Instructional Methods Selectively

Self-instructional methods can provide a most powerful means for learning, preparing for, initiating, sustaining, directing, and guiding good performances. Intentionally instructing yourself as to what to or what not to do and when and how to do it can help you perform at a higher level of excellence with greater consistency. But self-instruction is by no means a panacea to insure good performance. It is only one ingredient for success, and you have to learn when and how to use it to enhance performance. At times, it can be problematic as well.

When performing a well-learned skill with proficiency, instructional self-statements interrupt, interfere, and inhibit smooth, quick responding. Here focusing your attention on what you are doing and using images to "program" the desired execution are preferable to using verbal guidance.

Self-instructions emitted following performance may benefit future performances. The more distant such future performances are, however, the more likely these self-instructions will merely serve as precursors to self-criticism, impaired self-esteem, and even depression.

Instructions greatly enhance preparation. However, chronic self-instructions serve as internal prods, constantly driving you to perform. Self-instructional thoughts often imply the importance of doing well. When this thinking goes beyond motivating and directing performance to demanding and commanding desired performance, you put too much pressure on yourself, running the risk of encountering performance anxiety and setting yourself up for harsh self-criticism when performance falls short.

Use self-instructions. They are invaluable. But use them selectively, as suggested by this section. Self-instructions are most useful when they stimulate action, describe the appropriate responses, and delineate the order in which responses should be performed. I will describe ways of practicing and applying self-instructional methods, but first let's look at some of the other methods available for thought control.

COUNTERING

"The only sure weapon against bad ideas is better ideas"[11]

WHITNEY GRISWOLD

If you are not performing up to your desired standards, more than likely your cognitive behavior is actively contributing to your problem. Your confidence may be down. You might have lost sight of your goals or discounted their importance. Your goals may have been unrealistically high. You might have had difficulty maintaining your concentration. You may have given in to pain, fatigue, boredom, or temptation too easily. Nervousness or anger may have interfered with performance. Or perhaps you simply were not adequately prepared. In any case, if you performed poorly, it is a good bet that something was afoul with your thinking. If not explicit self-statements, then your perspective, beliefs, and appraisals affected how you dealt with each situation.

Once you have identified the kinds of thinking that interfere with your athletic performance, you can devise some strategies for coping with them. One viable strategy is to use this increased awareness to spur the deliberate utilization of better thought patterns. As you recognize some of your thoughts as dysfunctional, you can use them as a signal to intentionally plug in some of the more beneficial thoughts you have identified or to employ self-instructional methods. Often self-instructions alone will do the trick.

Many of your negative thoughts, however, have strong underlying bases. They habitually occur because you are used to filtering various situations through layers of rules, beliefs, assumptions, and perspectives you have about that situation, yourself, the world, and life in general. The private meaning with which you view and interpret events tints what you perceive just as though you viewed things through colored glasses. Similarly, you react to and interact with events, actively shaping your world based on "where you are coming from" and how you sort things out. As a result, thoughts and images that interfere with performance may be pervasive and quite resistant to change. Self-instructional methods might not do the job, or if they do work, they may work only temporarily. The problem may keep cropping up.

You probably can recall many instances where you unsuccessfully applied self-instructional methods (without calling them that) in an attempt to cope with negative thinking. You may have said to yourself, "I can't do this" or "I can't make it," then instructed yourself to "pick it up," "stay with it," or "hold on," only to come back with "I can't." Or perhaps in practice you have caught yourself thinking, "I don't want to do this," tried to tell yourself to "get after it," but merely went through the motions—or told yourself to "blow it off" and subsequently split.

It is difficult to get yourself to do something (even when employing self-instructional methods) if you really believe you can't do it. Nor are you likely to maintain motivation if deep down you do not believe your efforts will yield success. In instances like these, it may not be enough to direct your thoughts toward desired actions. You may first have to build a case against the underlying beliefs or perspectives that keep getting in your way.

One useful method of turning your thinking around is called countering. Countering is a kind of internal debate where you challenge and dispute the thinking that interferes with good performance. Countering consists of actively fighting your negative thoughts with facts and reason: counters. Counters are your ammunition for shooting down the misguided and inappropriate thinking that impedes successful execution.

Discover Any Hidden Meaning

In order to counter negative thinking successfully you must first know what it is you are countering. By identifying the thoughts that precede, accompany, and follow particularly poor performance you begin to be able to restructure it. Sometimes, however, this thinking is merely the tip of the iceberg. The thoughts that you heard yourself think convey implicit messages and/or are based on some underlying beliefs and perspectives that have to be countered if you are to bring about lasting changes. These hidden meanings must be discovered. For it is the meaning of your thoughts, not the explicit verbalizations, that must be countered.

When I was coaching swimming at the University of Texas, Felipe Muñoz (the 1968 200-meter breaststroke Olympic Gold Medalist) was on the team. Occasionally he would miss morning practice. When confronted with his absence he would inevitably respond with something like "Coach, I tried. But, Claire, she no let me go. She hug me and say: 'Felipe, don't leave me. Stay here with me.' Every time I try to get up, she pull me back into bed with her. She felt so warm and comfortable. I could not go." (Only toward the end of the school year did we find out that "Claire" was Felipe's pillow.)

Like Felipe, most of us have had conversations with our warm bed and pillow, or at least debated with ourselves over getting up in the morning (especially for a demanding early morning practice). Much of what is said in an "inner dialogue" like this is difficult to counter without first specifying and making explicit the implicit messages and underlying beliefs and perspectives. For example, when the alarm goes off, you might reach over, turn it off, and tell yourself: "I'm tired, I think I'll sleep some more." That may be difficult to argue with. It would probably be an accurate assessment of how you feel. You could not very well counter that thought with "I am not tired" and believe it. On the other hand, you might ferret out the implicit message that "I can't get up when I'm tired" and counter that with "You can too. You have before. And it is important that you do it now. Get up!"

Similarly, the whole conflict is embedded with assumptions and beliefs about the situation, your ability to handle it, and its consequences. You may be assuming that missing practices once in a while will not matter because (a) one does not need that much practice in order to realize top competitive performance; (b) you are so good that it doesn't matter if you practice much at all—you'll still win; (c) you're so bad that practice doesn't matter—you'll still lose; (d) sleep is more important than practice and the night life is more important than practice; (e) you don't really care whether missing morning practice affects performance, because you don't care if you do well or not—or some other basic belief about the utility or importance of morning practice. Once you recognize that messages like these are implicit in what you are actually saying to yourself and/or the underlying bases for your thoughts, you are in a much better position to counter them and make some fundamental lasting changes.

Thus, you could counter these beliefs as follows:

(a) Perhaps! But even if that is true, each additional practice will contribute to increasing the odds of getting where I want to go. Anyway, what makes me think missing practice won't hurt. If nothing else, I'd be building bad habits. I could make missing practice a regular part of my daily routine. And I would be interfering with establishing good sleeping habits. I don't want to do that. Get up and get going!

(b) Bull! No matter how good I am I still need the training. The competition is tough. Anyway, I want to improve, not stand still. This kind of thinking isn't useful. It only makes me complacent. Get up and go to practice!

(c) That's right! I probably can't win if I don't practice. But there's no reason to believe I can't improve (and win) if I prepare well enough. Where's the evidence that just because I have performed poorly in the past, I need to continue to do so? That's wrong! I don't need to perform poorly if I'm willing to train! Go to practice!

(d) OK, I'm tired. But I can go train in spite of the tiredness. If practice is a little harder this morning because I'm tired, maybe I can use that as a reminder to get some sleep the next time I'm tempted to stay up late. Sleep may feel more important now because I'm tired. But that's the tiredness talking. I want to reach my goals, so practice is important. Being tired isn't that terrible. But thinking that it is doesn't help. Get up!

(e) Yeah! It's easy not to care when you're tired and hurting. But that's a cop-out. Think how much you cared last time you did poorly. You don't want to feel that way again. Hit practice. It'll be worth it. You know you'll be glad you did. You always are. Get to practice!

Countering Rhetorical Questions

One of the most difficult thoughts to counter in its existing form is a rhetorical question. Rhetorical questions mark a definitive statement or opinion under a seemingly inquisitive thought. When you ask a rhetorical question, you are not really looking for an answer or an exploration of possible options. Instead, you are expressing an opinion or asseveration about the situation.

Sticking with our example of the conflict surrounding attempts to arise for morning practice, you might ask yourself, "What difference does it make if I miss one practice?" If you take that as a question, you are then left thinking of all the possible ways it may or may not make a difference. On the other hand, recognizing that it is a statement reflecting an opinion—that missing one practice probably will not matter—more readily leads to countering. Thus, you can tell yourself that "missing one might not matter, but I don't want to take the chance. And anyway, if I give in now, it makes it easier to give in again. If that happens often, it very likely will matter!" Discover what you really mean when you ask yourself a rhetorical question. A clearly stated opinion can be countered readily. Rhetorical questions only hide the problem.

Changing Beliefs by In-Depth Countering

Changing your way of thinking does not come easily. How you view things is firmly entrenched in well-learned ideas and perspectives. That is why it is so important to carefully ferret out messages implicit in your thinking and the underlying bases for these thoughts. Then you can carefully and vigorously debate and dispute these ideas in depth. Only after consistent, careful, and detailed challenging of these ideas, with lots of evidence and logic, will your beliefs begin to change. Then once you have convinced yourself intellectually of the fallacious or useless nature of such thinking and have generated new more useful perspectives, your thinking habits, emotional reactions, and behavior will gradually become more appropriate. This, of course, will benefit performance.

Naturally, the more evidence and logic you have on the side of your counter, the more believable and effective it is likely to be. And the more firmly you believe your counter, the less time it will take to turn your thinking around.

One thing that you have working for you when countering is that the evidence is on your side. Remember that you are only employing counters in situations where performance falls short (or where you catch yourself thinking in a way that interfered with performance in the past). Since your thoughts significantly affect performance and your performance is subpar, there is probably something wrong with your mental approach to the situation. The content of your thoughts or your reasoning process may be incorrect. At the very least, these cognitions are not useful.

With that the case, countering can begin by challenging the accuracy of your thinking with questions like "Is this thinking correct?" "Does it conform with reality and the rules of logic?" "Where is the evidence that _____?" "What makes me think that _____?"

Sometimes your thinking will be neither right nor wrong—it will be nonverifiable (impossible to prove). Then challenge the utility of your negative thinking, countering these thoughts with the evidence that they are not helping you reach your goals. Ask yourself: "Is this thinking in my own best interest?" "Does it help me perform efficiently and productively?" "Does this thinking help me feel the way I want to feel, or is it upsetting me and keeping me tense?" "Does it help me feel OK about myself?"

Once you have challenged the accuracy and utility of your own way of thinking, you can counter with statements along the same line. Thoughts such as "That is not correct," "Not true!" "Who says?" and "Wrongo!" directly attack and dispute the accuracy of incorrect thinking. And counters such as "That thinking is not useful," "This doesn't help me," "Big deal!" "Not relevant," "Who cares?" "So what?" "That thinking only gets me doubting myself," "This isn't helping my confidence (motivation)," "This isn't helping me feel the way I want to feel," and "That kind of thinking isn't helping me get along with my coach (teammates)" contest the utility of irrelevant or negative thoughts.

Your negative thoughts are usually stronger at first than your counters. You have been thinking that way for a long time. So it is important that you muster all the evidence you can to refute your old ideas and to support your counters.

It requires repeated, conscious, purposeful countering to replace old thinking habits with new. Thus, you best initially explore your thinking at a time designated solely for such work—a time when you are removed from the situation and free to debate the issues with yourself in great detail. By asking yourself questions like those that follow you build a case that makes your counters and your new, more useful perspectives more believable:

> "Where is the evidence that missing one practice won't hurt?"
> "What makes me think I can blow off practice and still reach my goals?"
> "How does it follow logically that just because I am tired, I can't get up and go to practice?"

Gradually, as you become more aware of the faulty and unproductive nature of your old perspectives, you can be more direct and concise, effectively reorienting your thinking with counters such as "Wrong!" "So what?" "Big deal!" "Why should I?" "That won't help me reach my goals," and "Why can't I?" without any further debate.

Notice that rhetorical questions often make good counters. "So what?" is an effective counter for the anxiety-producing "What if . . . ?" It implicitly suggests that even if the worst occurred, it would not be terrible or intolerable. Likewise, "Why can't I?" challenges your doubts about your ability to complete a task successfully and discounts the logic of generalizing about your adequacy on the basis of poor past performances.

Countering will help nullify the potential problems of negative thinking and get you back on track. But it will take active, vigorous, and persistent countering to replace your old ideas with new ideas and perspectives that will better help you perform well.

LABELING

A *label* is a word or short phrase descriptive of a person or event. Labeling is an important part of interpreting and bringing meaning to our world. We can use labels to sort out, classify, and even enrich our experience. Unfortunately, labeling can also shade our experience disadvantageously.

Labels carry many connotations and value judgments that influence what you attend to, how you feel about it, and whether you approach or avoid events. If you label something "good" or "good for you," you tend to seek it out. Such labels lead to pleasant feelings such as joy, happiness, and eager anticipation. If you label something "bad," you tend to avoid it. These labels lead to experiencing unpleasant emotional reactions such as anger, sadness, or anxiety. Extravagant labels such as "awful" or "terrible" often lead to inappropriate actions and excessive emotional responses.

Labels shape our expectations, influencing what we do. This is particularly true when we use labels to describe what we think is the cause of events. Labeling a noise in the night as the wind elicits considerably different action than does attributing that noise to a burglar. Similarly, labeling the way you felt in the water during warmup as "I don't have it today" has different ramifications for the upcoming race from attributing those sensations to soft water.

Particularly consequential are the labels we apply to people, especially ourselves. Our culture teaches us to view people as having personality traits, drives, emotions, and abilities which explain their behavior. Though these labels conveniently describe wide ranges of behavior, too often we inappropriately jump from using these terms as descriptive of some acts to using them as a cause of that and similar acts. This kind of misuse creates pessimism about being able to change. Labels seem to lend permanency to all they imply. If you see yourself as a competitor, you are likely to perist to face of a temporary setback. Obviously, this would not be bad. On the other hand, if you label yourself as a failure, you are more likely to give up following temporary defeats. A pregame lack of physiological arousal might be labeled calm·confidence, prompting good performance. Conversely, it might be labeled indifference, leading to a casual approach to the game.

Labeling often reflects capricious assessments and overgeneralizing, even though its consequences may be severe. Splashing in a puddle would hardly make someone a bird, but being slow to get a joke can sure make someone a "turkey." One poor performance can make someone seem "over the hill." One important dropped ball can make someone a "choker" or a "loser" despite a great career. (Ask Jackie Smith or Mickey Owens.)

Notably arbitrary and impactful is the "goodness" or "badness" we ascribe to people and events. Events are neither inherently good or bad. We label them that way based on social learning, whether we find them pleasurable or aversive, safe or dangerous, useful or dysfunctional. Mostly, however, such labels are arbitrary and definitional. This is not necessarily bad. In fact, labeling is a convenient tool for sorting out a complex world. The particular perspective you select, however, has major implications for goal attainment. In light of that, you often do well to question the accuracy and utility of some of your labels. If they are not useful, you may want to do some relabeling.

Relabeling

Merely relabeling an event, sensation, or personal quality can bring about extensive changes in behavior. If you attribute a poor performance as due to a "lack of effort," you are more likely to get after it next time than you are if you label it "bad luck." If a poor tackle signifies nothing more than a "poor tackle," rather than an "off day," you can still salvage the game. Similarly, by relabeling the physiological arousal you worriedly have called "nervousness" an "eager anticipation," you can transfer avoidance motives to a feeling of confidence.

Discarding and Avoiding Labeling

Labeling people (particularly yourself) usually is not useful, nor is it correct. Labels are static, people are ever-changing. Labeling people inevitably involves overgeneralization. By taking a single act such as failure as a sign of total incompetence you employ erroneous logic. Such labels mold expectancy and become self-fulfilling prophecies. You probably won't learn anything from a "bad coach." But everyone has something to offer, and no one is consistently bad. If you are someone who "can't serve," you will probably never improve. But, if you "frequently have hit bad serves," you can learn to hit good ones more often.

The permanency and self-fulfilling prophecy aspects of labeling makes complimentary labels more beneficial than disparaging ones. But universal evaluations and categorizations of several performances or abilities might better be discarded or avoided altogether. Rating and labeling performance helps give you direction for reaching your goals. Behavior can be changed. But you need to know when and how to change it. More global personal ratings, such as "I am good," "I lack confidence," or I am a failure," have less value. Pejorative labels lead to hopelessness, despair, self-consciousness, and blaming. And while flattering labels may enhance confidence, sooner or later they are likely to bring about complacency, one-upmanship, and self-oriented rather than task-oriented thinking.

PUTTING CHAMPIONSHIP THINKING TO WORK

The first step in championship thinking is increased awareness and understanding of the issues involved: a sort of consciousness raising. You need to understand that you are always actively engaged in cognitive activity, that the specific nature of this thinking impacts everything you do, and that although your thoughts often arise spontaneously, they can be controlled. You need to become aware of what you are thinking, to recognize what thoughts are awry, and to know what cognitions are more useful.

Throughout this chapter we have explored these issues. We have looked at the ubiquity of cognitions; the relationship between thoughts, behavior, and feelings; and some issues relating

to the content of thoughts. We have seen how some kinds of thinking work to inhibit good performance. And we have looked at
thinking tools—namely self-instructional methods, countering,
and relabeling—that can directly support your athletic efforts. In
subsequent chapters we will continue to examine carefully how
certain kinds of thinking affect your performance and what to do
about it.

Recognition and understanding of these issues are an important part of controlling your athletic fate. But they are not
enough. You need to know how to employ this knowledge. And
you need to apply what you have learned actively, vigorously,
and persistently.

Championship Thinking can be intentionally produced and it
can work just as well as if it occurred spontaneously. You can
purposely think in a way that directly aids performance. In doing
so, you blockade performance-impeding thoughts. And you can
fight unchecked negative thinking with deliberate employment of
adaptive thinking. With practice, consciously emitted useful
thought patterns may become as habitual and automatic as previous negative patterns.

Write It Out

By monitoring and listening to your thoughts and by following
the suggestions in this book, you can identify the material with
which you want to work. It is important to write it out. Careful
restructuring and rehearsal will hasten your progress. If you
merely work on championship thinking when you happen to
think of it (or recognize the need), relying on your memory, you
will probably make improvements much more slowly.

Writing it out helps you to specify clearly and verbalize
vague feelings, images, implicit messages, and underlying beliefs
and assumptions. Rewording thoughts and deriving suitable substitutes is much easier this way. You also provide yourself with
a stimulus for intentionally emitting championship thinking.

Mental Rehearsal

Habits are built partially through repetition. Rehearsal of new
thinking patterns, consisting of explicitly helpful self-statements
and reflecting more functional belief systems and perspectives,
can be the beginning of constructing new, more functional thinking habits.

One method of rehearsing useful self-talk is to write out specific statements and to read them to yourself. This can be of particular use in building confidence with affirmations (see Chapter 6). It is of utmost importance here (as well as with any intentionally produced thinking) that you attend to the content of what you are saying to yourself, emitting the accompanying effect and intention to comply with the self-statements. If you read thoughts or think these statements to yourself in a relatively mechanical or rote fashion without the accompanying meaning and inflection, you are likely to gain little from your efforts. You know how sometimes when you are reading, you suddenly realize you have no idea what you have just read? You have been running your eyes across the words, saying them to yourself, and turning the pages. But your thoughts were elsewhere (or you were in a daze). You were not paying any attention to what you read. So you have to read the last three pages all over again. Merely parroting a set of self-statements in a rote fashion has the same effect. You have to listen to, understand, and really mean what you say to yourself.

In Your Own Words

Attending to and meaning the thoughts you are rehearsing is aided by making sure they are in your own words. Your idiosyncratic manner of speaking holds the most meaning for you. Your expressions, cue words, and jargon are the vehicles for communication. Only you know if "bad" is bad or good, whether "right on" or "tough it out" is dated or still has some meaning, if the thought "popcorn" elicits actions, or whether "descend" means to go lower or faster.

Practice What You Preach

Just repeatedly reading or thinking prepared self-statements can be helpful in the beginnings of cognitive change. At least by thinking a certain thought you open yourself up to attend to evidence that can validate these statements and bring old beliefs into question. But there is a big difference between saying something to yourself and believing it. Mere repetition of positive thoughts is unlikely to fashion miracles. However, realistic, behavior-oriented self-statements coupled with action and backed by logical justification and empirical evidence can contribute to significantly rewarding changes.

Logical justification enhances the meaning of intentional self-talk. Thus, countering can be extremely effective in changing beliefs. Confirmatory evidence, however, is more powerful in influencing belief or attitudinal change. Thus, if you chronically think, "I am a worker" while loafing through practice, the thought will have little effect. While if you think "I train well," draw on evidence from past instances where you have trained well, and proceed to demonstrate a concentrated effortful performance on your next practice drill, you are likely to establish a situation where your thoughts stimulate effortful training performances and your training performances stimulate self-predictions of hard training in an equally escalating fashion. It works both ways. Thought elicits action and action elicits thought.

I once did an experiment to see the effects of thinking one brief "positive," "negative," or "neutral" statement had on swimming performance. The men on the University of Texas varsity swim team were randomly divided into three matched groups based on the results of a time trial. Then, a second timed swim was performed with one group instructed to think "I feel great," one group "I feel lousy," and one group "Utah is the Beehive State" to themselves after each turn and again in the middle of each lap. As predicted, the positive-thinking group on the whole performed significantly better than the other two, with the negative-thinking group performing the worst. However, the swimmer who performed best of all was in the "negative" thinking group. Upon questioning, he reported that he did as instructed but did not pay any attention to the designated statement he repeated to himself. He felt good going out. Then he caught a glimpse of the pace clock and saw his split. He knew he was moving. Though he "mouthed" the words as instructed, he also kept telling himself that he was doing well and felt good.

Many people seem to be extremely responsive to experiential data which support already held beliefs. It is all to easy to attend selectively to confirmatory rather than contradictory evidence. Thus, we tend to generate and revise our beliefs based on what we do. In *Cognition and Behavior Modification*, Michael Mahoney relates an anecdote about a mental patient who believed that he was dead:

> Frustrated in his efforts to dissuade the patient of this belief, a psychiatrist chanced upon a miniature experiment to settle the issue. He asked the patient, "Do dead people bleed?" "No, of course not," came the reply, at which point the psychiatrist quickly produced a scalpel and pricked the patient's finger. He stood quietly

as the amazed man watched a tiny drop of blood trickle from the incision. After an anguished silence and some obvious cognitive restructuring the patient looked up and remarked, "I'll be damned! Dead people do bleed!"[12]

When trying to induce a new thinking habit, prearrange for as many confirmatory experiences as possible and endeavor to act consistently with your desired thoughts. Actual performances congruent with the aspired beliefs frequently bring about dramatic and rapid changes. One way to control the desired results is to rehearse your thinking and coinciding actions imaginally (see Chapter 2). In imaginal competitions or practice you have complete control over what you do and how it turns out.

Scripts can be prepared that outline thinking likely to promote good performance under various practice, meet, or game conditions. These scripts then can be read or memorized and practiced imaginally or as the opportunity arises.

Whether practiced imaginally or in the actual situation, you can deliberately talk to yourself in a way that is most likely to lead to success. Well-directed self-talk will aid in preparation for the task prior to acting, guide you through performing, and help you to regroup when necessary. You can have prepared statements to think to yourself in preordained situations and a list of thoughts to plug in to get you back on track whenever things are not going according to plan. You can use any negative self-talk, undesirable feelings, or performance letdowns as reminders or signals to insert a prepared script.

Of course, the more you practice, the more automatically and effectively your new thinking habits will be employed. Though intentionally applied self-talk can be immediately effective, smoothly functioning thinking habits can take months, even years to develop. And your thoughts will never achieve perfection. Negative or dysfunctional thinking will slip in from time to time. But you can minimize the frequency of troublesome cognitions and minimize their detrimental effects when they do occur.

Neither is championship thinking a panacea. Your thoughts can direct attention, aid concentration, foster confidence, help you perform well under pressure, guide responding, help you cope with pain and fatigue, promote motivation, and help you to accurately assess performance for future good. But saying the right things to yourself has to be coupled with appropriate action. There is no free lunch.

2
IMAGINAL PRACTICE

Round about what is, lies a whole mysterious world of might be, a psychological romance of possibilities.[1]

LONGFELLOW

Imagination is limitless. It can take you places you have never been. And it can provide you with ways of getting there. Imagination frees you from limits imposed by time, habits, and the physical environment. In it lies a free and easy way to open new horizons. Yet it is real enough to pave the way to actually getting there.

When you imagine something vividly your body responds almost as if it were real. If you picture yourself running, swimming, hitting a ball, making a catch, or the like, small contractions can be measured in the muscles associated with these movements. As such, you can get the "feel" for the desired performance by doing it imaginally nearly the same as you could through actual practice. Thus, you can create practice experiences through imagination.

In recent studies it has been found that imaginally rehearsing such skills as free-throw shooting, dart throwing, and ring tossing improved performance. When imaginal practice was combined with physical practice, performance levels far exceeded those attained when either method was used alone.

THE ADVANTAGES

Increased Opportunity

Of course, imaginal practice cannot provide the physical conditioning derived from rigorous physical training. But it can help to prepare you to get the most out of your training sessions. And it provides an important adjunctive method to physical practice for skill development and refinement.

In the absence of opportunity to train, skills that might otherwise deteriorate can be partially or wholly maintained through imaginal practice. In "Athletes and Self-Hypnosis," Lee Pulos reports that Robert Foster, a former national rifle champion, imaginally practiced his shooting 10 minutes a day for a year while on noncombat duty in Vietnam. "Upon return to the United States, and with practically no actual practice with his competitive rifle, he entered a national meet and broke his own world record."[2] Similarly, imaginal practice can help keep your skills sharp when you are injured or otherwise have no access to the playing field.

The almost limitless nature of your imagination, the short time needed for imaginal practice, and the fact that you require nothing except imagery skills affords you greatly increased opportunity to create practice experiences.

In a golf tournament you are not allowed a practice shot. Yet Jack Nicklaus says he takes an imaginal one every time. In his book *Golf My Way* he reports:

> I never hit a shot . . . without having a very sharp, in-focus picture of it in my head. It's like a color movie. First I "see" the ball where I want it to finish, nice and white and sitting up high on the bright green grass. Then the scene quickly changes and I "see" the ball going there: its path, trajectory, and shape, even its behavior on landing. Then there is sort of a fade-out and the next scene shows me making the kind of swing that will turn the previous images into reality.[3]

When you are too tired to sensibly put in any extra physical practice you can always do it right imaginally. Bruce Jenner reportedly used imagery at home every evening to rehearse for his decathlon events in preparation for the 1976 Olympics.[4]

Learning theory suggests that the greater the similarity between practice conditions and test conditions the greater the transfer of learning. Yet practice situations rarely simulate closely the conditions of a big meet or game. If nothing else, it would be extremely difficult, if not impossible, to assemble competitors and large crowds so that you can better prepare for the game. Coaches try. They are aware of the importance of preparing for the actual situation. So football coaches, for example, often have one squad run the plays that the upcoming opponent is likely to use. By putting this team against the starters in practice, they better prepare the first team for the game. Some coaches play tape recordings of boisterious crowds so that scrimmages better approximate game conditions. It helps, but it is not the same thing. On the other hand, to the extent that you can anticipate the conditions of an upcoming event, you can duplicate them imaginally.

Most big meets or games only come once or twice a year. Events like the Olympic trials and the Olympics only arrive once every four years. This does not afford much opportunity for the practice gained from experience. And if it is your first time, you have no opportunity for such practice prior to the actual situations. Yet practice performing under pressure situations is important. You don't want to approach these rare opportunities tentatively or distractedly. As Emerson once said, "A great part of courage is having done the thing before." It would be near impossible to simulate the intensity of the competitive conditions faced in events like the Olympics or the Olympic trials, but you can do the thing before, and many times, through imaginal practice.

Similarly, your imagery skills allow you to prepare for unusual situations. You might travel north to practice for a game in the snow, travel south to prepare for the heat, or hope the weatherman will bring you some rainy days so you can practice just in case. But you would probably do better to spend a few moments practicing imaginally to handle these possible contingencies.

Full Control

When utilizing imagery, you have full control over what happens. This allows you to structure these imaginal practice sessions completely to your benefit.

Here you have a rare chance to get others to behave exactly as you want them to. In your imagination your opponents cannot do anything unexpected. And you can be certain they will set the occasion for you to work on the particular areas you want to. For example, you can practice getting out in the lead in a race and fending off your rival's late kick. You can practice going out behind and making a move. You can go neck and neck, trying out a move at different stages of the race. You can practice beating someone on the turns. Or you can simulate a touchout situation at the finish. All of these race variables can be practiced imaginally with full cooperation of your competition.

You also have full control of the results. Your performance can turn out exactly the way you want it to. This can bolster confidence. It really helps to get familiar with success experiences if you are to believe you can get the job done.

With your imagination, you can control for rain, the heat, various levels of wind, the glare of the sun, the lighting of the arena, as well as any other aspect of the physical environment. Based on some knowledge of the conditions you are likely to encounter, you can prepare yourself for any contingency.

In the heat of competition your habits endure. When practicing imaginally you are less likely to perform unthinkingly. You more easily can control what you do. In this way, you can forge new habits, practicing until you respond in the desired fashion automatically.

On those rare occasions when you do lose control of your imagery and replay old bad habits, you can stop and do it over. It is so easy to catch yourself, if you are doing it wrong imaginally, and, in milliseconds, reset the scene and try again. "Do-overs" are luxuries afforded by imaginal practice. They are rarely as available during physical practice and virtually never during competition.

Occasionally, some athletes even have difficulty ridding themselves of bad habits imaginally. No matter how they try, they seem to imagine themselves performing in the same old way. There are ways around this with imaginal techniques that cannot be done in actual competition. You can imagine someone whom you have seen perform in the desired fashion performing as you want to perform. Then, as if your body had no solid substance, you can imagine yourself climbing into your model's body and "going along for the ride" as the two of you perform correctly. As your model takes you along through the performance, experience how it feels to move in that way. Imagine this scene repeatedly. As you get the feel of it, imagine taking more and more responsibility for the movements; so that you are helping more and more. Gradually take over. Move from "going along for the ride" to taking your model along as you do all the work. Finally, move on to a solo performance.

I recently worked with a diver who could not get a reverse two-and-a-half. No matter how she tried, she always came up short. She could not even complete the dive imaginally. I had her pick out someone whom she had seen do the dive well. In this case, we had a film available of her model doing the dive. While watching the dive on film she imagined how it would feel. Then she imaginally climbed inside her model and did the dive with her. Over and over again they did the dive together, until she could imagine she was doing it with the model along for the ride. In a short time, she was not only able to clearly imagine herself doing a reverse two-and-a-half, but she was able to do one.

Slow Down Time

In athletics you often are required to respond so rapidly that it is impossible to think about what you are doing while you are doing it. Likewise, complex movements must be performed so quickly that it is nearly impossible to isolate the feel of their component parts. If you could slow things down, you could explore the experience more intensely and practice it with much greater attention to detail. In that way, you could build habits that could be performed quickly and smoothly in response even to the most subtle cues.

Unfortunately, when you slow down your actual movements, or slow down the competitive situation as it unfolds, it almost always alters the movement itself, the feel, or the competitive environment. You could slowly move your golf club through a predesignated path, but it would require tension in your arms that would not exist in a quick, smooth swing. You could practice hitting a slow curve ball, but its arc would be affected by gravity and air resistance differently than would a fast curve. And there is absolutely no way you could do a dive in slow motion while in the air and still complete it . . . except imaginally. On the other hand, you can rehearse imaginally any movement or competitive situation in slow motion and still maintain the integrity of the experience. Like a slow-motion videotape, the event develops exactly the same as at its normal speed, but you are able to attend to and process much more information in much greater detail.

Different Perspectives

Imagination affords you a means for viewing your performance as a participant, as an observer, or as a participant-observer. During performance your perspective is from the inside looking out. In imaginal practice you want to replicate that experience as much as possible. By practicing what it looks, feels, and sounds like to participate, you enhance your ability to perform well automatically under competitive conditions. Most of the time, this "participant" perspective is what you want to achieve during imaginal practice. There are times, however, when it behooves you to take a perspective that is different than the one you get during the real thing.

Sometimes it is useful to observe your performance. The magic of film and videotape allows you to see what you look like as you perform. This can be a tremendous aid to any athlete, but is crucial in sports like diving, gymnastics, figure skating, and other sports where what a judge sees may be as important to the outcome as what you do. You not only need to know what you are doing, but what you look like while doing it. Yet while our technology has advanced, it still has its limitations. The camera can only capture what you do. Your imagination can develop a picture of what you might do and what you want to do even though you have not done it yet.

By taking the view of a participant-observer you can use imaginal practice as a diagnostic method. Imaginally replaying past performances, you can pay attention to what you did wrong and/or particularly well. An assessment utilizing imagery is much better, for example, than trying to cover your man while you are thinking about the placement of your feet (for example, as in basketball, lacrosse, and football). It does not interfere with play. Yet imaginal practice allows you to view and feel your performance at the same time.

THE TECHNIQUE

When practicing imaginally it is important that you approximate actual experience as much as possible. The closer your images are to the real thing, the better the transfer of learning.

Make your imaginal practice as rich an experience as possible. Employ all your senses. And make your images as vivid and detailed as possible.

In actual competition, most people rely heavily on "feel" and sight. It is important that these sensations are recreated vividly during imaginal practice. Many people naturally employ clear visual images. Others tend to think more in words than in pictures. Some people do well in imaginally experiencing kinesthetic and other "feeling" cues. Few people, however, are adept at imaginally employing all their senses. Yet practice utilizing all your senses is important in simulating competitive situations. If nothing else, the sounds, smells, sights, and so on are necessary for accurately setting the scene. Fortunately, imaginal skills can be developed and refined through practice.

You could jump right in and start working on scenes designed to enhance your athletic performance. I would recommend, however, that you begin with some more emotionally neutral scenes that allow you to focus on developing your imaginary skills without being distracted by what the scenes connote.

There are many exercises that can enhance your ability to imaginally employ your senses vividly. I will present a few. Feel free to creatively develop your own. The important thing is that you work on your ability to visualize, willfully, vividly, and in great detail, the desired situation—and that you practice! A good beginning exercise for developing visual imagery is as follows:

> Close your eyes. Allow yourself to relax. . . . As you relax, imagine a blank screen. . . . On that screen visualize a blue circle. A rich and deep blue. . . . Now, let the blue circle gradually fade into a green one. . . . Then, allow the green circle to change to yellow. A smooth, shiny, solid, bright yellow circle. . . . Let the brightness fade out of the yellow and see the color change to a dull amber and on through orange to a deep, dark, rich red. . . . Scatter a bunch of small drops of blue in the red circle and watch them bleed into the red, mixing more and more evenly until the circle is a uniform purple. . . . Now let the purple get darker and darker until it becomes black. A dark, shiny, bottomless black hole. . . . Take the edges off the black circle and square them off so that your black circle becomes a black square. . . . Let the black become gray, gradually getting lighter and lighter until your gray square becomes white, leaving you with the white screen with which you began.

The next exercise allows you to get involved in hearing, smelling, tasting, and feeling the experience as well as visualizing a scene:

> Once again get comfortable, relax, and close your eyes. . . . Then, imagine a pitcher of fruit punch sitting on a kitchen counter. The pitcher is about three-quarters full. It has been sitting on the counter for quite some time, so it is room temperature. . . . Stick your index finger into the liquid. Notice the movement as your finger breaks the surface tension, causing waves of ripples to spread out, bouncing off the inside walls of the glass pitcher. Notice the feel of the punch: wet, tepid, and perhaps slightly sticky with some sugar. . . . Now bring your finger toward your mouth. . . . The fragrance of the punch on your finger precedes the taste as the remnants of liquid settle on your tongue. . . . Reaching into a bucket of ice you fill your fist with ice cubes. Your fingers chill at the touch of the cold, moist ice. . . . Holding your hand over the pitcher, you release the ice into the punch. In slow motion, the cubes fall into the liquid, splashing it up. . . . Picking up a long stirring spoon, you stir the punch and ice to cool it off. As you do, listen to the clang of the spoon against the pitcher and watch the whirlpool of colored liquid you have created. . . . Removing the spoon, lift the pitcher and pour yourself

> a glass of punch. . . . Be sure to notice the flow of the liquid in great detail as it fills the glass. . . . Next lift the glass and drink the contents. Really experience how it feels to taste the punch . . . savor the flavor. . . . Feel it pass through your throat, as you swallow, . . . and follow the cool liquid as it descends through your esophagus and into your stomach. . . .

Practice scenes also can be less structured. You can start with a basic setting and see what happens:

> Imagine that you are at home in your living room. . . . Look around and take in all the details. . . . What do you see? . . . What objects are there? . . . What colors do you see? . . . Notice the shape and the texture of the furniture. . . . What sounds do you hear? . . . Really be there, looking out. . . . What is the temperature like? . . . Is there any movement in the air? . . . What odors do you smell? . . . Use all your senses and take it all in.

Repeatedly practice completely throwing yourself into images such as these, experiencing them as if they were real. Use other objects and a variety of simple experiences to develop and polish your imaginal skills. As you get good results, begin to introduce objects and situations relevant to your sport. Most of you, if not already proficient, will be able to create richly detailed images in a short time with only a few minutes of daily practice.

Remember that you want to capture a total experience. Employ all your senses. Look for sounds, odors, colors, and especially the sights and feel of your imagined scenes.

A good test of your imagery skills is to be able to get a physical response from your body. If you can raise goosebumps or get a chill by imaginally diving into a cool pool or stepping outside to run on a cool day; if you elevate your heartbeat or begin to sweat as you imaginally strain to pick up some extra yardage—then more than likely your images are approximating the real situation very well.

Some of you will require little practice before you will be ready to employ imaginal practice for rehearsing performance situations. Others will require much more practice. Everyone, however, can achieve an adequate level of proficiency with which to make good use of imaginal practice.

Troubleshooting

As mentioned above, some people tend to think more in words than in pictures. If you find it difficult to get clear visual images, you still may be able to get clear images of sounds, smells, taste, and touch. In any case, imaginal skills can be acquired, developed, and refined.

One method of working on your skills is to use props. For example, if you had difficulty with the first exercise presented (on color), you might help yourself by prompting these same images with pictures. Get yourself some white sheets of paper. Place colored circles on the white sheets and use them to stimulate the images. Look at the circle. Then close your eyes, holding on to the image as long as you can. Don't be disappointed if you hold the image only briefly. With practice you will be able to increase the time span. Anyway, most scenes you will want to employ to rehearse athletic performance will consist of rapidly changing images.

You can use all sorts of visual stimuli to enhance your visualization skills. Pictures of the desired performance, photos of the setting, or your sports equipment are particularly good props for this purpose.

Similar strategies can be utilized for increasing your ability to imaginally employ other senses. You can ring a bell, click a light switch, or even play some music; then recreate the sounds imaginally. You can raise your arm to shoulder level, shoot a jump shot, or swing a bat; then imaginally reproduce the feel. Watching a videotape of your previous good performance can provide the impetus for repeated practice of successful execution. As you watch the tape, fuse yourself with the image. Feel it as you watch.

If your expectations prevent you from even imaginally performing in the desired fashion, you can use films (or live performances) of others as models. Imaginally performing as if you were that person, imagining you are that person as you actually perform, or imaginally fusing yourself with someone else as they perform or as you watch them on film (as described above) helps you get beyond those impasses caused by your self-imposed limitations.

Don't get discouraged if you don't seem to be making any progress. It may take many repetitions before you start to see results. But take heart. Even if you never get to the point where you can produce crystal-clear images, you still can derive subsantial benefit from imaginal practice. Thinking your way through the action works very well. You might want to write out a script for the situation and read it to yourself. In fact, I recommend doing so in preparation for imaginal practice even if your imagery skills are highly advanced.

PUTTING IMAGINAL
PRACTICE TO WORK

When the time comes for the competitive event, you want to be ready. You want to let it flow automatically. But the automaticity of response that constitutes being "in the groove," "on your game," or having the "winning feeling" requires a fine-tuning of psychological and physical factors. Consistent, hard physical training combined with regular imaginal practice will produce the smooth, easy-flowing actions that yield this performance excellence.

I recommend daily imaginal practice. Use these practice sessions to rehearse the acquisition of skills, correction of errors, and improvement of performance levels. Employ imaginal practice to bolster confidence, enhance concentration, and strengthen motivation. Utilize imagery skills to develop your ability to perform well under pressure and to perform well in spite of pain and fatigue. Apply imaginal practice to rehearse managing anger and frustration. And avail yourself of imaginal techniques to set the scene for researching thought control.

The best approach to imaginal practice will vary with the momentary desired focus. If you are concerned with motor skill development, practice getting the feel of the perfect movement or play. Begin with a written description of the desired action, a set of photos, films, or videotape. Then imaginally go through these specified movements in slow motion as well as at normal speed. Imaginal practice is particularly effective for complex tasks where the whole movement or the entire play can be incorporated into finely detailed slow-motion movements. Repeated imaginal practice will help your body to make the moves you want to make, comfortably and automatically.

Ideally you will get this mental preparation in long before a major competitive event. Then when it really counts you merely need to put it on automatic. By imaginally setting the scene for performance realistically and in great detail, you not only hone your skills, but you build the foundation for smooth good performance under even the most extreme conditions of competition.

If you are working on changing techniques, you may want to use imaginal practice for assessment purposes. Correction of errors often necessitates an analysis of the problem. The magnified view provided by a slow-motion imaginal replay can be an extremely useful device in isolating the feel of the technical error. By isolating and exaggerating the feel of the error, you can make it easier to get and practice the feel of performing the correct movement.

If you are interested in enhancing concentration, your imaginal scene will focus on those cues that facilitate performance under competitive conditions. Thus, a pitcher might practice visually picking up the sight of the catcher's glove at a specified time in his windup. Or a diver might rehearse locating her cue to open up. Similarly, you can learn not to attend to events that will distract from performance. For instance, a basketball player can practice having all other visual stimuli blur into the background while the basket looks crystal-clear and magnified as she shoots free throws. So too can a golfer practice tuning out everything but the line of his putt and the cup. A quarterback, on the other hand, will want to practice an efficient method of scanning the field to pick up any open receivers.

When imaginally practicing your physical moves, perform them correctly. Repeated experience of proper physical execution facilitates mastery. On the other hand, most of the psychological aspects of performance are better handled with *coping images,* where you imagine a problem beginning to develop, you catch it, plug in more adaptive responses, and handle it well. Allow your images to contain problems (you will face imperfection in competition), but always imagine successfully handling each situation. Practice bouncing back from poor performances, regaining confidence, handling bad breaks, adjusting to unexpected events, and so forth. This will involve rehearsing plugging in the thinking skills presented in Chapter 1 in a variety of imaginally set circumstances. In this way you will be more likely to maintain or regain a "winning attitude" automatically as your "mental errors" become cues to signal better championship thinking.

Imaginal practice can be done virtually anywhere and at any time. At night right before you go to sleep is a good opportunity for such practice. Your imagery skills are enhanced by relaxation. And relaxation will support a more restful and easily acquired sleep. A routine of relax, rehearse, relax, and sleep provides numerous benefits. You might use this time to include some scenes relevant to the next day's activity. For example, you might select goals for the next day's practice and program them imaginally. Or you might rehearse your strategy for the next day's competition.

Sometimes, imaginal practice will get you so geared up that it will be more difficult to get to sleep. If you extend your imaginal practice scenes to include a cooling-off and calming-down period, however, and follow them with some relaxation, you will facilitate the onset of sleep.

Bedtime is a convenient time for imaginal practice, but don't neglect other occasions. You can imaginally practice your moves, grooving good performances and correcting poor ones, during pauses in training: between shots, between repeats or drills, and so on. Or you can combine imaginal practice with other activities. With imagination you can inject yourself into an event you are watching on TV, using others' performances as props for your practice.

You can combine your imaginal practice with your physical practice. Imagery can transform a boring, repetitious drill into an exciting major athletic event. Consider how much easier it is to get motivated to put out a concerted effort if a practice session suddenly becomes the world championships. Creatively experience the *action*. But keep your imaginal practice out of the actual competitive performance. Rehearsal is for preparation. When the event presents itself, employ what you have already prepared.

Notice the emphasis is on practicing the action. Fantasizing about successful results is just that: fantasy. Rehearsing the performance (physically and imaginally) can transform those wished-for outcomes into realities. But it requires persistent, diligent, and conscientious practice!

Throw yourself into it. Make your imaginal practice an engaging, vivid experience. Immerse yourself in the scenes as if you were there. Actually be there in the most realistic way possible. The more realistic and vivid the experience, the better the learning.

IMAGES VERSUS WORDS

It is often said that a picture is worth a thousand words. So too has the emphasis in most work on imaginal practice been on visual images. Gallwey, for example, asserts that "images are better than words" and tells you "to program . . . with images rather than instructing yourself with words." The choice between images and words is not, however, quite that simple.

It is true that language has its limitations. It is difficult to describe comprehensively a scene or an action without losing some of its flavor no matter how eloquently expressed. Even when someone seems to succeed, it often is because the words evoke images. Moreover, words can be cumbersome. Try to describe gymnast Kurt Thomas's floor exercise routine. Better yet, imagine him trying to describe it while executing it!

Images clearly have some advantages. When you visualize a scene you can use the picture as a gross outline while selectively attending to details. There is a lot of information that need not be processed or attended to in order to support good performance. With images you save time, better replicate the experience, and more readily ascertain the relevant parts while maintaining the "whole picture."

Nevertheless, verbalization has its advantages, too. Perhaps the greatest is its propensity for generalization. Visualizing an event and talking about it involve very different processes. Images provide a more concrete representation of specific events. As a result they seem to lead to minimal generalization. On the other hand, words are more abstract representations of events. They seem to set the occasion for greater generalization, better preparing you for similar situations.

In any case, you will think! Self-talk is a ubiquitous part of your experience, sports or otherwise. As a result, you do well to develop both your imagery and self-verbalization skills.

Superlative athletic performance stems from a complete integration of human ability, physical and psychological. Recent neuropsychological research suggests that the dominant side of the modern human brain is more verbal than visual, while the nondominant side is given more to pictures than to words. Full utilization of psychological capability must incorporate both visual and verbal instructive and rehearsal techniques. Imaginal practice best includes words and images!

3

RELAXATION

Everybody performs better when he's relaxed.[1]
DAVE KINGMAN

It is tempting to present relaxation as a panacea. It is not, of course, but it is a wonderfully useful tool. It has been employed to combat stress, to temper anger, to treat ulcers, to combat menstrual cramps, to relieve insomnia, to alleviate headaches, to foster weight control, to alleviate anxiety (precompetitive anxiety, test anxiety, speech anxiety, social anxiety)—and the list goes on and on.

Not only does relaxation effectively lend itself to widely divergent remedial applications, it also can be effectively employed preventively and promotionally, further enhancing already good functioning. Relaxation training has been used to promote assertiveness, creativity, concentration, confidence, and problem solving. Moreover, it is a highly pleasurable state. The final product is physically, emotionally, and cognitively enjoyable. Even training and practice in relaxation procedures is highly pleasurable. Most importantly, for our purpose here, it can be an invaluable tool for enhancing athletic performance.

Relaxation is a skill that can be readily acquired by anyone. Following the procedures to be outlined, you can become skillful in its use in a few weeks.

Although relaxation is purposefully and actively employed, it is passively induced. Relaxation occurs in the absence of tension. It requires not doing anything. You must merely let it happen.

RELAXATION-TENSION
CONTRASTS

I recommend that you begin with a relaxation-tension contrast procedure. This technique is one of the better, if not the best, relaxation induction procedures. It also sensitizes you to the contrasting feelings of varying amounts of tension in your muscles. In this way, you learn to better control the appropriate muscle tension and relaxation that facilitate maximally good physical performance. In addition, increased muscular tension often is a sign of performance-debilitating anxiety. Learning to read your body and recognize these tensions can be the first step in controlling competitive anxiety.

The relaxation-tension contrast procedure consists of systematically tensing and relaxing various muscle groups of the body one at a time. By contrasting what it feels like to be tense with what it feels like to release that tension and relax, you will learn how to intentionally relax your muscles more completely and to achieve deep states of relaxation.

When one group of muscles is tense, there is a tendency to tense surrounding muscles as well. As you go through the alternate tensing and relaxing of the various muscle groups, try to localize the tension in the particular muscle groups you are focusing on. Keep the rest of your body as relaxed as possible. For example, one of the first things you will be instructed to do is to tense your biceps. When so instructed, most people tend to make a fist and tense the muscles of their hands and forearms, as well as their biceps. Don't do that. Instead, keep your hands and forearms loose and relaxed, letting your hands hang limply at the wrist.

The instructions to be presented are based on relaxation instructions devised by Joseph Wolpe and Arnold A. Lazarus, who have provided a model for many subsequent versions of relaxation training techniques. Mine are no exception. Wolpe and Lazarus's original instructions may be found in appendix 4 of *Behavioral Therapy Techniques*.[2]

The first couple of times you practice this sequence, you may want to have someone read it to you. Or you may want to tape-record it so you can passively let yourself be guided by your own voice. The instructions should include pauses of approximately five seconds where indicated by ellipsis dots (. . .). Relaxation training may be undertaken individually, or the instructions may be read to a large group (such as an entire team).

Initially, relaxation will be facilitated by a quiet setting where there are likely to be no distractions. Nevertheless, some distractions may arise, particularly if relaxation training is done in a group. Someone may come in late. Someone may sneeze, cough, or fall asleep and begin to snore. Don't worry about it. Notice it, then go back to what you are doing. Anyway, as you become more proficient at relaxation later on, you will want to arrange intentionally for practice to take place in a distracting environment.

Many people fall asleep during a relaxation sequence, especially if it is done lying down. If you do fall asleep, don't worry about it. It is not terrible. On the other hand, the purpose of relaxation training is to learn a skill that can be intentionally applied. If you fall asleep, it is difficult to acquire that skill. So pay attention to the sequence of tensing and relaxing the various muscle groups. If you notice yourself starting to drift off, refocus on what you are doing. (Or if you are being directed by oral instructions, refocus on the voice.) If you feel yourself getting drowsy, just reach up and gently rub your eyes.

Begin by getting yourself comfortable, lying down on a flat surface (a carpeted floor or an exercise mat works well). Remove eyeglasses or contact lenses. Loosen any tight clothing that might constrict circulation. Take off any rings, watches, or other jewelry you may be wearing.

Lie flat on your back, resting your hands at your sides. Do not cross your legs. Instead, let your heels rest flat on the ground. Now here are the instructions:

> Get comfortable and close your eyes. Keep them closed throughout the rest of the exercise. Now take a minute to finish whatever you have on your mind. Then concentrate on getting as relaxed as you possibly can. Don't worry about getting perfectly relaxed. Just get as relaxed as you can for today. Let yourself relax. (Pause for approximately one minute.)
>
> Now, as you relax like that, clench your right fist. Clench it tighter and notice the tension as you do so. Right hand tense, forearms tense. . . . Now relax your right hand. Let the tension dissolve as your fingers loosen up. . . . Feel that relaxation. . . . Now get yourself comfortable and let yourself relax more all over. . . . Once more, clench your right fist . . . tighter and tighter . . . look for the tension . . . study it. . . . Now let go. Relax. Let all the muscles in your right arm go loose and heavy. . . .

Now clench your left fist . . . tighter and tighter . . . keep the rest of your body relaxed as you isolate the tension in your left hand and forearm. Now relax once again. Relax more and more deeply. . . . Let the relaxation proceed on its own as you do nothing more than release the tension you had produced. . . . Once again, clench your left fist . . . hold it . . . observe the feeling in your left hand and foream. . . . Now relax. . . .

Now clench both fists . . . both fists tense . . . and relax. Let all the muscles in your arms become loose. Let gravity take over. . . . Clench both fists again . . . tighter and tighter. . . . Now relax both hands. . . . Notice the contrast in your feelings between when you tense up and when you relax. . . .

Now bend your elbows and tense your biceps. . . . Both arms up . . . now relax your arms . . . let your arms gently fall back into a comfortable and relaxed position, and become more relaxed all over. . . . Once more, tense your biceps . . . study the tension . . . and relax . . . just feel that relaxation. . . .

Now straighten your arms and tense your triceps . . . tense them harder . . . and relax . . . let the relaxation proceed on its own. . . . Once again, tense your triceps . . . tighter and tighter . . . notice the tension . . . and relax. Let your arms relax completely. Let go more and more. Even when your arms feel totally relaxed, let them relax even further. And let your whole body relax more and more deeply. . . . As you relax, you might feel a tingling sensation, you might feel a warm sensation, your arms may feel heavy, or you may feel so light that it almost seems like you are floating. Whatever you feel, notice it and go with it, relaxing deeper and deeper and ever deeper. . . .

Now direct your attention to your facial muscles. Raise your eyebrows and wrinkle up your forehead . . . wrinkle it tighter. . . . Now relax your forehead . . . feel a gentle wave of relaxation flowing over your forehead and scalp, smoothing it out. . . . Now frown and crease your brows . . . relax once more and notice the difference. . . . Now close your eyes tighter and tighter . . . study the feelings . . . and relax your eyes. Keep your eyes closed gently, comfortably, and relax. . . . Now crinkle up your nose, observe the tension. . . . Relax, and note the difference. . . . Now bite your teeth together and feel the tension in your jaws. . . . Relax your jaws, letting your lips part slightly as you do . . . just feel that relaxation. . . . Now push your tongue up against the roof of your mouth . . . and relax . . . appreciate the relief. . . . Now press your lips together . . . tighter and tighter . . . and relax . . . let yourself relax to the best of your ability. . . . Notice how the relaxation progresses more and more deeply as you do nothing but let go of the tension . . . just let yourself relax. . . .

Now shrug your shoulders up and feel the tension in your shoulders, neck, and upper back . . . relax your shoulders. . . . Now bring your shoulders forward and feel the tension that way . . . relax your shoulders again. Relaxing more and more deeply. . . . Feel the relaxation in your shoulders, neck, and upper back. . . . Relax your eyes . . . feel the deepening relaxation in your nose . . . cheeks . . . jaws . . . lips . . . tongue . . . and even down into your throat. . . . Let yourself relax. . . .

Now breathe in deeply and hold your breath . . . study the tension . . . now let the air out slowly, automatically, and relax. Continue to breathe normally, gently, freely, and relax. . . . Notice how each time you breathe out, you relax deeper and deeper. Go with it. . . . With each exhalation relax more and more deeply. (Pause approximately 30 seconds.) . . . Now take a deep breath. Then let the air out. Continue pushing it out, until your lungs are empty, then stop. Don't breathe . . . feel the tension and uneasiness from stopping your breathing. . . . Don't breathe. . . . Now breathe in. Breathe normally, gently, freely, and appreciate the relief. . . . Once again, notice how each time you exhale the relaxation progresses more and more deeply. . . .

Now, as you relax like that, press and tighten your stomach muscles as if you are preparing to get hit in the stomach . . . hold it, observe the tension . . . and relax. . . . Notice the sense of calm that fills you as you relax your stomach more and more. . . . Now push your stomach out as far as it can go . . . and relax your stomach. . . . This time, pull your stomach in, look for the tension . . . now relax. Relax your stomach fully . . . feel the waves of relaxation spread throughout your stomach, chest and upper back. . . .

Now tense your buttocks and thighs by pressing your heels down on the ground as hard as you can. . . . Study the tension. . . . Now relax your hips and thighs and note the difference. . . . Once again tense your thighs . . . and relax. . . . Experience the vast contrast in feelings in your legs as your muscles switch off, relaxing more and more. . . . Now flex your calves by pointing your toes . . . and relax your calves. . . . This time bring your toes up toward your face so that you feel tension along your shins. . . . Now relax again . . . keep relaxing like that . . . notice the heaviness of your lower body as you let all your muscles grow loose and you let gravity take over. . . .

Let yourself relax further all over . . . feel the relaxation in your toes and feet . . . spread the relaxation up your legs, over your ankles, calves and shins, knees, thighs, buttocks, and hips. . . . Let yourself relax more and more. . . . Feel the relaxation spread into your stomach, waist, and lower back . . . the waves of relaxation travel through your chest and upper back into your shoulders and arms down to the tips of your fingers, relaxing you further and further and ever deeper. . . . Feel the relaxation in your neck, throat, and mouth . . . feel the relaxation deepening in all the muscles of your face. Let yourself relax more and more deeply in your jaws, nose, eyes, brows, forehead, and scalp. Feel relaxed from head to toe. . . .

Now, in just a moment I will count backward from five to one. When I get to one you will feel relaxed and refreshed but alert and wide awake . . . 5 . . . 4 . . . 3 . . . 2 . . . 1.

As you went through the relaxation-tension contrasts procedure you may have noticed some parts of your body that were more difficult to relax than others. These difficulties are usually clues to areas in which you may be chronically carrying around a lot of tension. They also may indicate muscle groups where you are prone to get tense first when nervous or angry. Pay particular attention to these areas. Periodically check them out during the day. And check for tension in these muscle groups in situations where you notice some discomfort or think tension is likely to occur. If you find tension in these areas, just relax it away. If you have difficulty letting go of the tension, tense these muscles even more, then let go. This intentional tensing will give you greater control. As you let go of the newly increased tension you will get a better feel for relaxing these muscles and will be able to continue going with it, relaxing even further.

Common problem areas are in the lower back, upper back, stomach, neck, jaws, and around the temples or eyes. If you frequently get headaches, you may be carrying a lot of tension around in the back of the neck, in the jaws, or around the temples or eyes. If you tend to have a "nervous stomach," look for tension there. Some of you will find that you almost always walk around with your shoulders partially shrugged. Whatever your problem area (if any), closely monitor it until you get it under control.

In presenting the above instructions I have elected to follow closely the specific muscle groups designated for relaxation-tension contrasts, and the order in which the muscle groups are attended to, as presented by Wolpe and Lazarus. You need not use the same sequence. If desired, you can begin with the muscles of the face and work down, start at the feet and toes and work up, or begin with concentrating on breathing. These methods work just as well. Whatever way you elect to order the sequence of muscle relaxation-tension contrasts, stick with it the first few times you practice. Then, as you get more skilled, vary the muscle group with which you begin. This will initially allow for better learning, while subsequently promoting generalized effectiveness.

If you have gone through the above relaxation procedure or have had other experiences with relaxation techniques, you know that relaxation is a pleasant, peaceful experience. It feels good. That alone would make it worthwhile. But for our purposes that is not enough. Here relaxation techniques are presented as a means of developing a skill that can be employed to facilitate good performance. Like the development and maintenance of any skill, relaxation takes practice.

You should practice the relaxation-tension contrasts procedure at least once a day (preferably twice) for two to three weeks.

Then move on to one of the shorter techniques, foregoing the tensing entirely. I do recommend, however, that you return to a complete relaxation-tension contrast sequence periodically as a sort of booster shot.

My experience has been that most people can learn basic relaxation skills easily. Athletes in particular seem to acquire the skills quite rapidly and easily. They tend to be very aware of their bodies and well practiced in controlling them. Furthermore, results are often immediate and dramatic. This does not, however, lessen the need for practice. The ease with which you will be able to apply relaxation and the completeness with which you will be able to relax your muscles will be greatly enhanced with practice.

A good time to practice is in bed at night just before going to sleep. Here it is easy to couple practice of relaxation with practice of thought control and/or imaginal practice. Moreover, relaxation facilitates the onset of sleep. This fact makes such timing of practice convenient.

During the first week to week-and-a-half, practice inducing relaxation with the relaxation-tension contrasts procedure while lying down. Then intermittently introduce practice sessions where you go through the whole procedure while seated in a comfortable chair. This will help you to use relaxation as an active coping skill instead of merely as a pleasant interlude.

In addition to setting aside time specifically for practicing relaxation, you should begin right away to practice and experiment with plugging in relaxation as opportunities present themselves during the day. Plug in relaxation to help you deal with stressful situations, to quell anxieties, to temper anger, or whenever you begin to experience the tensions of everyday living. Employ relaxation to deal with precompetitive jitters, to help you get to sleep the night before an event, and to enhance functioning in a wide variety of potentially stressful situations that may or may not have anything to do with sports. Take particular care to practice plugging in relaxation in response to the signals your body gives you. Use physiological cues (such as the symptoms of nervousness, the feelings of pain or fatigue, and, of course, increased muscular tension) and cognitive cues (such as panicky thoughts, ruminative worrying, and flight of ideas) as signals to produce a relaxation response. The more you practice, the better you will get. And the more you monitor your body, picking up on muscular tension as it occurs and using it as a signal to plug in relaxation, the smoother and more automatically your relaxation skills will plug in.

PROGRESSIVE RELAXATION
WITHOUT ANY TENSING

With practice, you eventually should be able to relax completely in a matter of seconds merely by purposely letting go of the tension. The next step in training toward that goal is to learn to induce a state of complete relaxation without doing any tensing.

Prepare yourself as recommended for the relaxation-tension contrasts. Remove eyeglasses or contacts, loosen restrictive apparel, and so forth.

You may choose to go through the following procedure either while lying down or while sitting in a recliner or other comfortable chair. I recommend you intersperse both in your training. In either case, let your arms rest comfortably at your side with your hands on your lap (not on the arms of the chair, if sitting) and your heels flat on the ground.

Get yourself comfortable and close your eyes. Keep your eyes closed comfortably throughout the exercise. . . .

Now take a minute to finish up whatever is on your mind. Then concentrate on getting as relaxed as you possibly can for today. Don't worry about getting perfectly relaxed. Just get as relaxed as you can for now. (Pause for approximately one minute.)

Now as you relax like that, I want you to imagine a warm beam of light shining on a spot in the middle of your forehead. A warm beam of light hitting that spot in the middle of your forehead and sending penetrating waves of warm relaxation flowing through your forehead and scalp, smoothing them out. . . . Just feel the relaxation in your forehead and scalp . . . and flowing down over your eyelids and into your eyes . . . the relaxation penetrating deeply into your eyes, making your eyes feel very soft . . . relaxing you more and more deeply. . . . Feel the relaxation flowing gently across your nose and spreading out across your cheeks. . . . The relaxation travels down your cheeks and into your jaws . . . feel the relaxation in your face and jaws . . . and let your lips part slightly as your jaws relax more and more deeply . . . just let go . . . let all your facial muscles hang loose and easy and free of wrinkles as the relaxation now spreads into your mouth. . . . Relax your lips and your tongue . . . and feel the relaxation even flowing deep down into your throat. . . . Let yourself relax. . . .

Relax your neck . . . and let the waves of relaxation spread into your shoulders and upper back, relaxing you more and more. . . . Spread the relaxation over your shoulders and down into your arms. . . . Feel the waves of relaxation traveling down your arms, flowing deeply into your biceps and triceps . . . across your elbows and into your forearms . . . the waves of relaxation penetrating into your forearms deeply massaging, soothing, and relaxing your forearms more and more. . . . Feel the relaxation flowing through your wrists, into your hands to the very tips of your fingers. . . . Your fingertips may begin to tingle, your hands may feel cool or warm—whatever you feel, go with it relaxing more and more deeply . . . relaxing further and further and ever deeper. . . .

Feel how comfortable and relaxed you feel . . . breathe easily and freely in and out . . . and notice how much more relaxed you become each time you exhale . . . each time you breathe out. As you breathe, you become more and more relaxed . . . and feel that relaxation spreading out across your chest and into your back . . . feel the waves of relaxation flowing around down your sides and down into your stomach and waist . . . and all the way through into your lower back in a warm, penetrating, wavy calm . . . a definite wave of calm . . . notice how secure and at peace you feel as you relax more and more . . . and deeper and deeper. . . .

The waves of relaxation spread down into your hips and buttocks . . . the relaxation flows into your upper legs, and as your thigh muscles just shut off, grow loose, and you let gravity take over . . . your legs feel heavy as the relaxation spreads across your knees . . . flowing down into your shins and calves . . . quiet and still and very, very relaxed . . . your legs may feel as if they are melting into the carpet [chair, mat, etc.] . . . the relaxation grows deeper and deeper. . . . Feel the relaxation traveling down your legs through your ankles and into your feet and toes . . . feel relaxed from head to toe . . . and feel the calm that goes with the relaxation . . . a good safe, secure feeling . . . a feeling of peacefulness . . . let yourself relax. . . .

Now in just a moment I will count backward from five to one. . . . When I get to one you will feel relaxed and refreshed, but alert and wide awake . . . 5 . . . 4 . . . 3 . . . 2 . . . 1 . . . when you feel like it, just open your eyes.

Progressive relaxation without any tensing should be practiced at least once a day for about two weeks following two to three weeks of practice in relaxation-tension contrasts. You might choose to be led through this procedure with oral instructions the first few times. After that, though, you should be able to lie (or sit) down and relax by starting at one area of your body (head, feet, or hands) and spreading the relaxation through your entire body without any external guidance.

Many people are able to get very good at achieving a deep state of relaxation through the use of progressive relaxation without any tensing or through imagery-based techniques without ever being exposed to relaxation-tension contrasts procedures. For the athlete wishing to use relaxation to directly facilitate performance, however, it is important to be well practiced in relaxation-tension contrasts. Sensitivity to varying amounts of muscle tension in sundry muscle groups is critical for the differential relaxation that maximizes speed, power, endurance, and fluidity of movement.

Continue to practice using your relaxation skills to ease discomfort, to cope with problems, and to enhance functioning as opportunities present themselves throughout each day. The more you practice, the better you will get at employing relaxation techniques and the greater benefit you will derive from such applications.

As time goes on and you continue to practice, you will find yourself relaxing more quickly, more easily, and more completely. The mere intention to relax will soon become ample prod to elicit relaxation. There are, however, some very useful shortcut techniques that can facilitate a quick, easy relaxation response.

BREATHING TECHNIQUES

A commonly used method of calming down is simply to take in a really deep breath, let it out, and relax. This works particularly well if you are attuned to the benefits of relaxation and well practiced at releasing muscular tension. Deep breathing then becomes a cue for going with the relaxation that naturally occurs with exhalation and taking it further, relaxing more and more deeply.

More stubbornly persisting tension can often be counteracted by filling your lungs a little bit at a time, holding it at each step, and then letting it out all at once. Thus, you take in a little bit of air, hold it a second, then, without exhaling, breathe in some more air. Continue this process until your lungs are completely full. Then exhale slowly, letting the air escape automatically. This method tends to exaggerate the feel of relaxation that accompanies exhalation, amplify the relief experienced with breathing out and then breathing normally, and distract you from whatever is causing the tension.

CUE WORDS

As described in Chapter 1, self-instructional methods are an effective means of eliciting desired responding. Especially as you develop your relaxation skills, simply instructing yourself to "relax" can be sufficient for evoking a relaxation response. Other cue words or phrases—"calm," "be cool," "mellow," or anything that holds an appropriate meaning for you—can bring on relaxation under various circumstances.

Particularly effective is the combination of cue words with breathing techniques. Take a deep breath. Let it out slowly. Then continue to breathe normally, gently, freely, and easily. Focus on your breathing and notice how each time you exhale you relax that much more. And each time you exhale, as you exhale, think the word "relax" (or another cue word or phrase of your choice) to yourself. Do that about 20 or 30 times without bothering to count.

In many circumstances you will not have the time to lie or sit down and go through an entire relaxation sequence. Or it might be socially awkward to do so. Nevertheless, in most situations you can take a minute to close your eyes, focus on your breathing, and repeatedly tell yourself to "relax" or "be calm" as you breathe out. And you virtually always can take a deep breath, let it out slowly, and tell yourself to "relax."

USE OF IMAGERY

Pleasant Scenes

Relaxation can be induced by imaginally placing yourself in a very comfortable, peaceful setting. Get as comfortable as you can. Try to let go of any tension and relax; then pick out one scene that is peaceful for you and imagine yourself there.

You might imagine yourself floating on a raft on a lake on a warm summer day, being gently rocked by the waves. You might select lying on a blanket on a tropical beach with a warm, gentle breeze softly caressing your body. Or you might choose to imagine yourself peacefully relaxing at home before a crackling fire on a cold winter's evening. Whatever you pick, really be there, looking out. Carefully attend to the scene in vivid detail. Use all your senses. Look for the various sights. Notice the different colors and shapes. Listen for the sounds. Be aware of the smells. And pay close attention to how it feels. Experience it all in a very calm, relaxing, and peaceful way.

Puppet on a String

Another effective technique for inducing relaxation through the use of imagery is Puppet on a String. Imagine yourself a puppet on a string. Imagine it is as if you have no muscles with which to make any movements and no tendons to hold your bones together. Instead, the various parts of your body are attached to strings. All movement is controlled by pulling those strings. All support comes from taut strings.

Now imagine all the strings are completely slack. All your body parts hang loose. You have no means of support against gravity. You collapse completely limp into the chair (mat, floor, etc.).

Ragdoll

A similar imaginally induced relaxation technique is Ragdoll. As in Puppet on a String, there is no potential for movement. Some people prefer Ragdoll, however, because of the soft feelings it tends to elicit.

Imagine you are a ragdoll. You have no muscles, no tendons, no bones. You are stuffed with fluff. You softly sink into the ground (chair, carpet, etc.).

Weightlessness

Imagine you are floating in a medium where there is no gravity. As in outer space, you have no weight. But unlike outer space, oxygen is freely available. You have no need to move and no need to support yourself against gravity which is not there. You can merely relax, freely float, and drift off into a comfortable, peaceful place deep inside.

DIFFERENTIAL RELAXATION

You can induce relaxation immediately prior to the performance situation via any of the above techniques. This is a particularly effective strategy for quelling nervousness, enhancing confidence and promoting clear, rational, task-directed thoughts as you prepare to compete. Relaxation can also directly facilitate the power, speed, endurance, and grace with which you perform. Toward these ends, training in differential relaxation is particularly efficacious.

Edmund Jacobson has defined differential relaxation as "the minimum of tensions in the muscles requisite for an act, along with relaxation of other muscles."[3] As such, differential relaxation has two key components. It is important not to overtense muscles you are using and to relax completely muscle groups not being used.

In order to produce maximum force, muscles antagonistic to the prime movers must be relaxed. You can easily demonstrate this fact to yourself. Bend your arm and tense your biceps. Tense them as tight as you can. Holding the tension, try to straighten out your arm. If you keep your biceps tense, you cannot do it. Now ease up on the tension in the biceps ever so slightly. Now try to straighten your arm. Depending on how much tension you have retained in your biceps you should be able to make some straightening motion, but only very slowly, with great difficulty, and much trembling. Now bend your arm again. This time relax your biceps completely. Then straighten your arm. Easy, isn't it?

Now hold your arm out straight and tense your triceps. Tensing your triceps as hard as you can, try to bend your arm. Again, you should not be able to do it. Now straighten your arm again and tense your triceps, but not quite as tense. Try to bend your arm. This time you should be able to do it, but only very slowly, with great effort and accompanied by tremors. This time hold your arm out straight, but relax your triceps as much as you can. Now bend your arm. Get the message?

Every movement you make is initiated and controlled by muscular tension. For every movement you can make there is an opposite movement controlled by muscles antagonistic to the muscles that control the original movement. For example, in order to bend your arm you have to tense your biceps. Straightening out your arm requires tensing of the triceps muscles.

Tension in antagonistic muscles interferes with the smooth functioning of needed muscle groups. This is often what happens when you try too hard. In an attempt to get maximum speed or force you not only tense needed muscles, but inadvertently tense antagonistic muscles as well, thereby putting an added strain on your body. Instead of using your muscles optimally, you end up pitting one muscle against another as if you were doing isometric exercises. That can only slow you down, weaken the force you can produce and tire you out. In fact, it can be so draining that athletes often report complete exhaustion after poor performances, while reporting that they feel as if they could have done better following their better performances.

Rarely, though, does anyone produce so much tension in antagonistic muscles that they cannot move, or have as much difficulty moving as experienced in the biceps-triceps demonstration (though some people do get frozen with fear). Nevertheless, any tension at all in antagonistic muscles can impede performance.

Many coaches in sports like track, swimming, and speed skating have begun to teach their sprinters to try to go at seven-eighths speed instead of all-out. Too often, an all-out effort seems to result in unnecessary tension that slows an athlete down.

Tension in antagonistic muscles interferes with fluidity of movement. The added stress of working one muscle against another may cause soreness or injury. And excessive tension contributes to early fatigue. Finally, excessive tension heightens awareness of the self-inflicted pain that accompanies effortful performance.

Skill in differential relaxation comes with increased sensitivity to varying stages of relaxation and tension in individual muscle groups and with practice in relaxing unneeded muscles while appropriately tensing needed muscle groups. The more control you can acquire and exhibit over tensing the needed muscle groups when appropriate and relaxing muscle groups not needed immediately, the better you will be able to perform.

The focus of differential relaxation training varies with the particular sport. In swimming, for example, freestylers and backstrokers work on alternately tensing one arm while relaxing the other. Butterfliers and breaststrokers work on alternately tensing and relaxing both arms simultaneously. These differential relaxation skills are then employed to make the recovery of the stroke as relaxed as possible, thereby conserving energy and delaying fatigue.

Divers and gymnasts do well to focus on relaxing the neck and shoulders to facilitate certain moves, while golfers can help their swing with differentially applied relaxation in the hips, waist, and back.

Athletes in all sports should place emphasis on learning to remain relaxed in the muscles of the face during performance. Tension in muscle groups not being employed tends to spread to nearby muscle groups, thereby interfering with the smooth functioning of those muscle groups needed. Grimacing with effort only tends to increase tension in the neck and shoulders, needlessly expends energy, and exacerbates feelings of pain and fatigue. It does not facilitate performance. Tension in the muscles of the face in no way enhances power, speed, endurance, or grace in any sport.

CONCLUSION

Relaxation is an active coping skill that is pleasurable, readily acquired, and of great benefit for you as an athlete. It can be employed to enhance confidence, to aid in concentration, and to promote a winning attitude.

Tense muscles and tense emotions go hand in hand. Fortunately, relaxation can be utilized to reduce precompetitive nervousness, to prevent or alleviate anger, and to help you remain calm at the perception of pain and fatigue.

Differential relaxation can be used to insure that optimal levels of muscular tension are not exceeded during competition. As a result, power, speed, flexibility, endurance, and fluidity of response are all aided by the appropriate use of relaxation.

Relaxation can serve to prevent some injuries. And it has even been utilized in attempts to promote and speed healing.

Finally, relaxation is tremendously useful in the practice of other psychological techniques for aiding athletic performance. A state of relaxation facilitates the use of imaginal practice and thought control techniques. It even helps set the stage for the imaginal practice of the appropriate utilization of relaxation skills.

4
GOAL
SETTING

I know what I want, just to run faster. Just to run faster.[1]

EVELYN ASHFORD

Floundering in the world of sports without setting goals is like shooting without aiming. You might enjoy the blast and kick of the gun, but you probably won't bag the bird.

Goals can be tremendously useful tools. When set correctly and employed properly, they can enrich your participation in sports. They can be used to direct your activities, guiding you toward your destination efficiently and expediently. And they can help keep you motivated, serving as fuel to power your journey. Furthermore, they invite total involvement, making the trip more enjoyable.

Yet goal setting can be a complex and often confusing endeavor. Much of the confusion surrounding goal setting stems from the fact that the term *goal* is used interchangeably in a wide variety of ways, referring to standards to be achieved, activities to be performed, rewards, desired states, or even motives. Furthermore, goals are set for today, this week, this month, this season, four years from now, your career, or even your lifetime.

Deciding what form your goals should take and what length of time you should set your goals for can be a formidable task. Let's see if we can sort it all out.

At one point, some of you made a decision to get involved in athletic competition. Perhaps you also decided to direct that involvement toward some purpose. You may have read about top-notch athletes signing multimillion-dollar contracts and decided you too were going to star as a professional athlete. Or maybe you saw Mark Spitz win seven Olympic Gold Medals and decided you wanted to win eight. More of you, however, probably got involved in athletics by chance, at the urging of others, or because you just happened to be there.

I started competitive swimming when I was asked to swim in a local town league meet in which my brother was competing. My parents had brought me along to watch. Our town's team, however, was short on the 10-and-under age group. So I was recruited. The next thing I knew, I was practicing regularly and swimming in meets.

Most of you probably had similar experiences. Your parents may have signed you up for Little League baseball, Pop Warner football, tennis lessons, golf lessons, or the like. Your friends may have been involved, so you wanted to join too. Or a coach may have thought you had potential and asked you to come out for the team.

Whether or not you had a particular destination in mind when you began, you do well to look at where you are now, where you are going, why you're bothering, and how you can get what you want efficiently and enjoyably.

WHERE ARE YOU GOING?

If you want to get the most out of your sports experience, it is important that you know where you are heading. You cannot make intelligent decisions about your involvement without some direction. If you have your eye on the Olympics or on a pro contract, your actions should differ considerably from what you should do if you want to lose weight, get some relaxation or recreation, or exercise for your health.

You may not have identified any purpose for your involvement in sports. You may just like to play. Obviously, there is nothing wrong with that. However, even if you are just along for the ride, you can often enrich your experience by having a destination.

Even when you have some direction, it is all too easy to get lost in what you are doing and lose sight of where you are going. When you are practicing every day it becomes such a habit that most of the time you are there because that's what you do at that time of day. Particularly if your team has rules about attendance (or if your parents take you by the hand every day, drive you to practice, and deposit you on the steps), you are likely not to think about whether or not you want to do it or why; you're just there because it is time for practice. Even if yours is a casual pursuit,

Wednesday might be tennis night. And you may get in the habit of showing up because it is Wednesday night, not because you want to play tennis. This kind of routine is not bad. In fact, it encourages regularity. On the other hand, if you find yourself routinely going through the motions of practice, you do well to reassert your goals, reminding yourself of why you are doing what you are doing.

At some time most of you probably have identified some goals for your participation in sports. Things do change, however. I think you do well to periodically review your direction by asking yourself where you are going and what you want to achieve through sports.

A good place to start is to ask yourself what you want to get out of your sport (tennis, golf, baseball, etc.). By clearly identifying what you want, you have a clearer basis from which to decide what standards you will have to achieve to get what you want and what you can do in order to have the best chance of accomplishing those standards of performance.

You might be interested in some material gains, like money or a scholarship to college, ribbons, medals, or trophies.

You might be interested in some physical by-products of exercising. You might anticipate feeling better: sleeping better, digesting your food better. You might think you will help yourself stay free of physical ailments, and maybe even live longer. You might anticipate looking better via better weight control and increased muscle tone. Perhaps you anticipate being able to do more because of increased strength and stamina.

Then there are affiliation and other social rewards. It's fun to be part of a group involved in group projects. Sports often provide an opportunity to make and maintain friends with similar interests and values, people with whom you likely have more to share. There's team unity, the feeling of working together toward some goal—and perhaps increased opportunities for flirting and dating.

Sports often afford the opportunity to travel. You may get to see new places. You get to do things in conjunction with meets or games. You can meet people from many different geographical areas.

Often most important is the intrinsic value. It just plain feels good to hit the ball right, to be loose and breathing easily, to have the rhythm of your stroke. The thrill of competition can be exhilarating. The feeling of mastery of a task or of the environment can be exciting. And the feelings of satisfaction that accompany making standards that you set for yourself can be great.

You learn and practice many skills. Time management, assertiveness, self-control (avoiding temptation and enduring fatigue, pain, or boredom), the contingent relationship between work and rewards, self-evaluative skills, teamwork, and so forth, all can be acquired through sports and readily generalized to other areas of your life.

You may be interested in prestige, publicity, or recognition. Or you may enjoy cooperating with authority: parents or coaches.

The important thing, however, is that you clearly identify some reasons for participating. This will serve to keep you motivated. The more reasons you have for being involved, for persisting at a task, or for performing with intensity, the more likely your behavior will remain goal-directed.

It is rare when an athlete has such solidarity of purpose that anticipation of one goal can keep him motivated. It happens. There are people who care about nothing in life except making the pros or winning the Olympics. These goals are enough to keep them working long and hard for years. But this is very rare. And there are problems associated with such a single-minded approach.

It is more likely that, sooner, or later, you will be dragging (from working so hard), you will feel bored, schoolwork or finances will be piling up, the weather will be cold and miserable, your boyfriend/girlfriend/spouse/lover will have just rejected you. Then, when faced with a tedious practice you will find yourself asking, "Why am I doing this?" At these times, if you want to help yourself stay on the road to reaching your goals, you need to be able to answer this question. You need to provide yourself with the self-motivation needed to go on, by reminding yourself of your goals and how what you are doing relates to reaching these goals.

The more reasons you have available to cite to yourself, the more likely you will be successful in keeping yourself motivated. Some reasons will work one day, but not another. Wanting to make the Olympics might keep you going sometimes, but other times a far-off, iffy proposition like that won't be enough. Those times you will need a shorter-term, more certain goal, like wanting to stay in shape.

The first step, then, in setting your goals is to identify the things you get out of participating, The things you would like to get, and the things that you might get and might find attractive. Think of as many as you can and write them down. Be creative.

Get ideas from coaches and fellow athletes, and make some up. The more reasons and rewards you have identified, the more likely you are to stay motivated.

Idiosyncratic reasons are appropriate. You need not identify "good reasons" (in someone else's judgment or based on some arbitrary standard). You merely need to identify good reasons for you. As long as they have some incentive value for stimulating goal-directed behavior, they are good reasons.

GETTING THERE: MAPPING THE WAY

Goals can be behavior-directing. Once you have established where you are going and what you hope to find when you get there, you want to find the surest, quickest route to follow. In essence, you want to map the way. By drawing a plan of things that you best can do, you increase the chances that you will reach your long-term goals.

Goals such as to be the best, to win an Olympic Gold Medal, to make the pros, to get a scholarship to college, or the like can be motivating. These goals are exciting and often inspirational. Unfortunately, what they most often inspire you to do is to day-dream about reaching them, while you sit idly, doing little or nothing to help yourself get there. These goals are important. They identify the destination picked for your journey. But they are not sufficient. They tell you little of how to get there.

Goals as Standards

Goals as standards specify some criterion level of performance you seek to attain. These type of goals include goals like to rush for 1,000 yards, to break a minute for 100-meter fly, to pole-vault 16'½", to break par, to win Wimbledon, to kick a 63-yard field goal, and to bat .300.

Standards clearly mark the criteria for evaluating performance. They give you something to strive for and a means of comparison for assessing your progress. Often the spoils of sports follow the attainment of set standards. And the feelings of accomplishment that come with reaching these goals is perhaps the most rewarding experience of all.

Many of you will have already set goals that were standards you wanted to achieve (like to break the world record, to qualify for the National Championship, or to make the team) without having identified the likely products of these performances. If so, it is important that you identify why you want to reach this standard, what it will mean to you when you do, and what it is you expect to get out of it. Otherwise, when reaching your goal, you may end up disappointed, depressed, or wondering what it was all for.

Specifying the rewards and standards you seek gives you a basis for further utilization of goal-setting techniques. It is a good start. It will help give you a good perspective, keep you motivated to train hard, and provide you with some direction for your efforts.

Pyramid of Goals

A road map can provide you with a relatively certain route to your final destination. The world of sports provides you with far less certainty. You cannot map out a plan that guarantees success. You can, however, specify a behavioral plan for getting where you want to go in a quick, efficient, and enjoyable way.

The major league prospect who wants to get in shape and make the team obviously enhances his chances more by doing wind sprints, playing pepper, taking batting practice, drilling a pickoff play, and so on, than by daydreaming about his major league debut. The daydreaming is useful, but only if it inspires some action.

Ask yourself, "What can I do in order to maximize my chances of reaching my long-term goals?" This will help you see if your present activities are in line with your ultimate goals. If not, it will help you restructure one or the other.

It is too easy to get lost in what you are doing and forget why you are doing it. The recreational tennis player who has a must-not-miss Wednesday evening game, argues line calls, and berates himself for missed shots has lost his perspective. A supposedly relaxing evening of tennis ends up generating more tension than it relieves.

Similarly, the serious competitor often finds it difficult to relate the drudgery, pain, and fatigue of daily practice to successful performances months or even years later. But by systematically outlining the steps leading to your long-term goals, you readily can demonstrate the connection between day-to-day behaviors

and future performances. Then you can outline a training
schedule that will best aid your quest.

For example, suppose you are a swimmer who wants to make
the Olympics. After identifying the elimination process through
which you must survive, you do well to ask yourself what you
can do to maximize your chances of getting there. The answer, of
course, in this example, would be to swim as fast as you possibly
can. You would then ask yourself what you can do to maximize
the chances that you would swim closest to your potential in the
critical races. In answering this question, identify what you can
do now to prepare yourself for these future performances. Thus,
you would ask yourself what would it take to swim faster. And
you would likely come up with answers like: increased speed,
increased power, increased endurance, increased flexibility,
improved technique, improved cognitive skills, and good health.

You would then outline a plan of action for each of these
goals. For example, to increase power you will want to do some
sprinting, pulling with paddles and tube, weight training, and
other dry land exercises. To increase speed, you will want to do
hypoxic training and sprinting. For endurance you might do some
interval training or long, slow distance training.

By working backward, in this step-by-step fashion, from your
long-term goals to setting goals for daily and weekly activity you
put yourself in a much better position to make intelligent decisions about what to do and not to do in order to be more likely
to achieve your long-term goals. And you also build in an awareness of how your daily workout behaviors relate to achievement
of your long-term goals. This will help keep you motivated. Runner Brendan Foster suggests that a concrete training schedule is
a motivating force. "By having a definite plan to follow," he says,
"you feel that each ten mile run through the rain is a specific piece
of the jig-saw, and not just another run."[2]

Of course, the more specific you can get about the behaviors
required to realize your long-term objectives, the more specific
you can get in setting goals for training. Thus, if you can estimate
how fast you will have to swim in order to make the Olympic
team, you can estimate how fast you will have to train. Subsequently, you can strive to train at least that fast.

For example, if you think it will take a 1:57 to make the
Olympic team in the 200-meter butterfly, you can train accordingly. A 1:57 would probably require splits of about :56 and 1:01
for the first and second 100s, respectively. So you would know,

for example, that if you could repeat five 100-meter butterfly swims on a 1:20 send off and hold 1:01 or better in practice, you would be confident of getting home in 1:01 in a meet.

Notice that you will specify a large number of behaviors that will be integrally related to reaching your long-term objectives. You might think of each of your goals as building blocks used to construct a pyramid of success. Each of these behaviors (or training goals) strengthens the foundation upon which you are building your pyramid. Omission of any of these behaviors or failure to reach any of these goals weakens the foundation. The pyramid might still stand up if you do not reach some of your goals. Each one you miss, however, weakens the structure. Success then can come toppling down.

Time Framework for Goals

It is often difficult to relate your immediate behavior to your final destination. As such, it may be difficult to maintain motivation. Rewards that may or may not be obtained at some far-off future date may not provide the incentive necessary to elicit present behavior (especially if that behavior is immediately unpleasant). By setting goals for each week's training, for each upcoming meet or game, and for the season, however, you can relate your immediate behavior to objectives that are closer at hand. These goals reflect what you can do *now* to impact attainment of your long-term goals. You can't win the Olympics now, if they are two years away. But you can prepare yourself through training. Realizing that "a journey of a thousand miles begins with but a single step" and that every day's practice brings you a little closer will help keep you motivated.

Like climbing a mountain, athletic progress can be slow and difficult. Sometimes you will take the wrong way. Other times you will lose your grip and slide back down the hill a way. The thought of reaching the crest may be enough to keep you going through the pain, loneliness, and struggles of the climb. You can make the climb easier and more enjoyable, however, by setting checkpoints (short-term goals) along the way. There you can pause and enjoy the view. You can see how far you have come. And you can judge the best way to go from there.

Similarly, the road to the pros or the Olympics is long and hard. (And you may very well never get there.) But constantly striving for and reaching shorter-term goals can help make getting there half the fun. Who knows? It might very well be more worthwhile. As Lord Houghton said, "The virtue lies in the struggle, not the prize."

Specific Behaviors

The more clearly your goals are specified, the better they guide your trip to your destination. Vague, nebulous goals are like poor directions—they make it harder to find your way. Well-specified behavioral goals clearly define the route to be taken.

Most of you, however, have been conditioned to think in more general terms. As a result, you would more probably set goals such as to play more aggressively, to be more confident, to get stronger, to lose weight, or to improve attitude. While all of these are worthwhile goals, in the form they are in they are not very useful.

For example, what does it mean to "play more aggressively"? Although everyone has some idea of what constitutes "aggressive play," it is doubtful that any two people could agree 100 percent of the time on their definitions. And your conception of "aggressive play" probably would vary from instance to instance. On the other hand, you could specify what you mean by "aggressive play." For instance, charging the net after a serve might be considered aggressive tennis. Or taking the lead in the first 100 of a 500-meter freestyle might be designated as an aggressive swim.

Similarly, you would be hard-pressed to "be more confident." You could, however, increase the frequency with which you predicted good performances to yourself (thought confidently), told others you would do well (spoke confidently), or relaxed immediately prior to an important event (looked and felt confident).

Your coach may want you to "improve your attitude." But it is difficult to improve your attitude unless your coach clearly communicates what behavior he wants changed. For one thing, what you think attitude entails and what your coach thinks it means may not agree. Your coach, however, could specify clearly the behaviors he infers your attitude from. Then you would know what to do. For example, your coach might want you to demonstrate a better attitude by arriving at practice on time more frequently, by hitting a tackling dummy harder, by spending longer periods of time practicing putting, or by disagreeing with him less often.

By specifying goals more clearly in terms of behaviors to be performed you can break down larger, unwieldy goals into smaller, more manageable units. You tell yourself what to do. You also give yourself an immediate objective that you can work on *now*. In a sense, you bring your long-term goals closer. In these ways, you increase the odds that you will realize your long-term goals.

Go back over your goals and reword them so that they specify particular behaviors to be performed. It is important that your training goals reflect what it is you are to do. While in the long run you may want to increase strength, win a medal, or get a scholarship, you want to specify what it is that you can *do now* to facilitate achieving those ends.

Make Your Goals Positive

Word your goals in a positive direction. That is, identify things to do instead of things not to do. Telling yourself not to do something does not work as well. It just calls your attention to the undesired act. If you have ever been on a diet, you know that reminding yourself not to eat sweets is an almost guaranteed method of having the thought of sweets preoccupy your mind.

If there is a behavior you want to reduce in frequency or to eliminate, set your goals to do some alternative, incompatible behavior. So instead of setting a goal not to arrive at practice late, set a goal to get there on time. It is much easier to focus your efforts with success on doing something than on not doing something. And the techniques to be employed in trying to increase a behavior are usually more pleasant.

Set Measurable Goals

Your goals should have a clearly specified, measurable standard of performance associated with them. You are going to want to know when and if you reach your goals. The only way to insure that knowledge is to quantify your goals.

By attaching numbers—units of measure—to clearly specified goals you enable yourself (or someone else) to measure your progress against this standard. In this way, you will give yourself a clear-cut means for comparing your actual performance against your desired performance. You will be able to assess whether or not you are on the right track. This will help safeguard against mere good intentions, against continuing with nonproductive behavior, and against abandoning viable strategies because your very real progress has gone unnoticed.

Set your goals as behaviors to be increased or decreased up or down to some specified, numerically quantified standard of performance within a certain time framework. Thus, instead of setting a goal to "improve my attendance at practice," you do better to set a goal to "attend at least nine of the eleven scheduled practices this week." Instead of setting a goal to "run more," you do better to set a goal to run "at least twenty-three miles this week." Instead of "working more on my long field goals," set a goal to kick "at least five successful field goals from forty-five to fifty yards and three from over fifty at least three days this week." Instead of deciding to "work on my putting," decide to "make at least one hundred successful putts at least three days this week."

Build in Success

Goals should specify behaviors to be performed at some quantified level of performance within some specified time framework. But what level of performance should your standards reflect? How high should you set your goals?

It is best to strive for a fairly steady progression of success experiences. Notice I said "fairly steady." Temporary setbacks are inevitable. Human beings are fallible. (Yes, even you!) As a result, substandard performances will occur. There is no way around it. You do want, however, to succeed as often as possible. You also want to minimize the number and size of setbacks. Continued success will foster continued interest, enjoyment, motivation, and confidence. Let's face it. It's more fun when you are doing well. You are also more likely to do well when you are having fun. That's a nice self-escalating spiral to get caught in.

Your judgments about how well you are doing more than likely will be based on how your actual performances compare with your goals. You can build in success by making goals readily attainable with concerted efforts.

Set goals that are progressively more desirable (this usually means more difficult to achieve).* You want to continue to improve

*The jogger or swimmer who runs or swims to keep in shape may be content to maintain a certain distance and frequency for exercise. Nonetheless, there are other areas

and make progress toward your goal. But even the smallest incremental improvements should be cause for celebration. Depending upon the time framework within which you are working, as long as you are making progress you want to encourage persistence. The pleasure of reaching your goals can provide this encouragement.

Set your goals so that they reflect readily attainable, progressively more desirable standards. Of course, the only way of really knowing if a goal is realistic and attainable is by whether or not you actually reach it. However, you can make some good guesses based on the level of your past performances and your previous rate of improvement. You usually do well to set goals that specify standards of performance a little better than you have been achieving.

The size of the incremental increases in standards you best set will depend on your progress to date. If you have been improving rapidly, you might set goals for fairly large incremental improvements. If you are improving slowly or seem to have leveled off, you do well to look for the smallest of improvements.

When you are just starting out in a sport, you are likely to improve rapidly as you acquire the rudimentary skills. As you become more proficient and perform better, progress becomes much harder to earn. Improvements may come slowly and in small increments. But even the smallest incremental improvements in performance may make the difference between winning and losing, a Gold and a Silver, or the finals and the "banana heat."* Set your goals accordingly.

You might think of your progress as similar to the progression of a pole vault competition. The lowest height is likely cleared by large margins and by most competitors. As the competition goes on, the bar is moved up by smaller and smaller

---

where recreational pursuits benefit from improved performance. Enhanced technical excellence often promotes increased enjoyment of any sport. It is more fun when you perform more efficiently and effectively. Though I swim competitively and enjoy it, my main motivation is to maintain my conditioning, muscle tone, and weight. Nevertheless, the harder I train, the more I enjoy it. When in top shape, I can do things that I cannot otherwise do. Those activities are tremendously exhilarating and enjoyable.

*In the 1975 NCAA swimming championships, Fred Tyler and Lee Engstrand finished the 200-yard individual medley together. The scoreboard showed their times as tied to the one-thousandth of a second. However, the electronic timing system judged places to the ten-thousandth of a second. Thus, Lee Engstrand missed the NCAA 200 I.M. championship by less than one one-thousandth of a second.

increases in height. As the bar is raised, the margin with which the bar is cleared generally gets smaller, until there is little or no clearly visible space between the vaulter and the bar as he goes over. Also, as the height is increased, the number of misses increases. Similarly, the percentage of times your performance improves will decrease, and the size of your improvements will generally decrease, as you become more and more proficient at your sport.

If your goals are too high and you consistently fail to reach them, you may get frustrated, discouraged, down on yourself, or quit. Weightlifter Phil Sanderson says, "You need a goal that takes one step at a time. . . . Too many lifters set unrealistic goals for themselves and then drop out when they fail to achieve them."[3] Even perceiving your goals as being too difficult can program in failure. When you believe you cannot succeed, you are more likely to give up or not even attempt to work at it. You are likely to think there is no use in trying. Whereas if you set your goals so as to insure a fairly steady progression of success experiences, you are likely to promote enjoyment, maintain interest, and persist in your journey to excellence.

Program in success by keeping your goals reasonable. Set goals that reflect small incremental improvements on past performances. For example, if you have been completing five reps (repetitions) at 195 pounds on a bench press consistently for two weeks and four reps before that, you might set your goal to do at least six reps at 195 next time. If the last four times you swam a 500 freestyle you bettered your best time by approximately 5 seconds, you might reasonably set a goal for your next 500 to go at least 5 seconds faster than your best time. But be careful. If you go 3 or 4 seconds better than your best time, are you going to be disappointed at your best-ever effort? You might be better off aiming for a performance "at least faster than" your previous effort.

Don't Limit Yourself

Goals have a way of determining levels of performance. Just as aiming at a target helps determine the general area in which you shoot, goals can largely determine a range within which you perform. On the one hand, this is desirable. You want to know where you are going and the best way to get there. Goals can do this job. On the other hand, goals can unduly limit your performance.

Obviously, there are realistic limits to what you can do *at this point in time*. But some goals put a ceiling on what you are likely to achieve. Be careful to set goals that will not preclude extraordinarily good performances. Leave the door open for you to make sizable improvements.

How many teams won the Super Bowl their first chance? Well, Green Bay did (but then, someone had to win the first one), and San Francisco did, but someone also had to win that game between two first-timers. Joe Namath and the New York Jets did, and the Pittsburgh Steelers did. That is all. Everyone else got beat their first time out. There are probably lots of reasons why: nervousness, the party atmosphere, and so on. However, I think part of the reason is that teams set their goals to get there. But once they have been there, playing in it isn't enough. Now they want to win.

At the 1978 National USS Short Course Swimming Championships, Nick Nevid, a virtual unknown who had just barely made qualifying standards, burst onto the national scene by defeating NCAA champion Scott Spann and Olympic Gold Medalist John Hencken to win the 200-yard breaststroke. Nick's victory represented only the second time a swimmer had won a national AAU title in his first national competition.

United States swimming is tremendously competitive. Just making cutoffs for Nationals is a monumental achievement. Because of that, most swimmers set their goals to make it to Nationals, without giving much thought to what they are going to do when they get there. It is not until they have experienced it once that they begin to set their sights on Gold.

Even the movies' Rocky Balboa limited himself by setting his goal to go the distance. Granted, Rocky is a fictional story. But in Rocky II, when he set his goal to win rather than to go the distance, he won the championship.

There is nothing wrong with setting goals like getting to the Super Bowl, making the Nationals cuts, or going the distance. But you do well to plan for what you want to do when you reach that goal. Set some goals to prepare you for the next step. Once you get to the championship, be prepared for a winning effort.

And keep the door open for superlative efforts. If you set a goal to run under 4:00 for the mile and you make it, you are likely to go a 3:59.9 or thereabouts. If you set your goal to go at least under 4:00, you may be opening the way to a 3:57 or even a 3:55. Such open-ended goals permit major breakthroughs.

Build in success with realistically attainable, progressively more desirable standards. But make these open-ended steps. Set your goals to at least achieve some standard. You want to be pleased with realistically small increments in performance, but strive for huge gains. High but realistic goals encourage more fruitful outcomes.

This is particularly important in training. Most athletes will strive for that superlative effort in the meet or game situation. Unfortunately, far too many athletes are content to exert moderate effort in practice.

In training you are free to give it your all. If you are a swimmer who has never made a series of 10 100-yard repeats on an interval faster than 1:10 and you try a set on 1:05, what do you have to lose? If you don't make it, fine. You move back over to the 1:10 lane and finish the set. But you tried. Maybe next time you will get it. If you do make it, you are one step closer to your meet goals.

On the other hand, in a meet you only have one chance. If the meet isn't too important, you might try going out considerably faster than you ever have before. Unless you have made the big gains in training, however, going out that fast is likely to take its toll. You will probably have trouble getting back and you will probably end up with a slower time than if you had controlled your pace.

You don't have to wait for the meet to make major breakthroughs. In fact, you do well to strive for them in training. If you make them there, the meet performances will more realistically follow.

Be careful not to limit yourself. Strive for perfection. Limiting what you think is possible can only defeat you before you start. It is best to strive to perform better than is seemingly possible, while still appreciating the more modest successes achieved along the way.

ASSESSING YOUR GOALS

Once you have set the full range of goals outlining your final destination, your reasons for wanting to get there, and your behavioral road map, it is important to go back over your goals assessing the viability of your plan. Ask yourself:

1. Are my goals realistic?
2. What are the odds of my reaching my goals?
3. Are my goals measurable?
4. Is the payoff worth the price?

5. Have I outlined a likely road to success?
6. How much control do I have over reaching my goals?
7. What opportunities exist?
8. Are there other ways of reaching my goals?

Are My Goals Realistic?

Often just writing out your goals will take care of unrealistic goals that you have been working toward but have not explicitly verbalized. The most common problem in this area is perfectionistic goals.

While you are unlikely to verbalize perfectionistic goals, you often behave as if you have set them. A baseball player would never expect to hit 1.000 for the year. Yet how many of you expect a hit each and every time up? Collectively you don't expect it. But how easy it is to forget that these collective statistics accumulate from individual chances.

What Are the Odds of My Reaching My Goals?

It is worth trying to estimate the odds of goal attainment. If your goals are readily attained, it can be encouraging. Those good odds also may give you the freedom to pay more attention to other goals, to try something more ambitious, or to just relax and enjoy the ride.

On the other hand, if reaching your goals is highly improbable, you can benefit from that knowledge, too. Noting that making the pros is a highly unlikely achievement can influence your behavior. You may choose to reset your goals. Or you may want to extend greater appreciation to the other rewards you can reap along the way in your quest for a professional career. If you choose to continue your pursuit in light of improbable odds, then you can specify some things you will have to do to increase your chances of success.

Are My Goals Measurable?

I have already emphasized the importance of quantifying your behavior goals. If you have attached a number to some clearly specified behavior, you will have no difficulty assessing whether or not you reached your goal.

Some of your longer-term goals can be inspirational and/or help direct your training efforts without being measurable. As such, they have value. At some point, however, they may present a problem. The knowledge that you will never know if you made it may take away your incentive.

Many of you will want to "play as well as you possibly can"—or to "reach your potential." But how will you know when you've played as well as you can or have reached your potential? When you no longer improve? Well, maybe! Or that might just mean you never got there and were over the hill before you got to the top. Presently, there is no known way of accurately assessing your athletic potential.

Some recreational athletes jog or swim because they want to live longer. You might increase longevity through exercise. Lately, there seems to be some evidence that this is true for the population in general. But for you, as an individual, it cannot be determined. There is no way of telling whether or not you will live longer because you exercised. Presumably, when you die you won't be able to compare your lifespan with an otherwise potential one. Even your survivors will have no means for comparison. However long you live, you live. There is no way of telling what might have been.

One of the most common problems in athletics is the equation of self-worth with performance. Many people think (at some level) that if they win the Olympics, make All-American, make All-State, make All-District, or whatever, they will somehow be better people. How good a person you are is nonverifiable. You can only measure it arbitrarily by definition. And it is futile and destructive to even try (see Chapter 6). Make sure that all of your goals are measurable. You will want to know when and if you achieve them.

Is the Payoff Worth the Price?

How many of you know who Bill Mulliken is? How about Jed Graef? Thompson Mann? Steve Rerych? Matt Vogel? All of these people won Gold Medals in the Olympics in swimming. For many of these athletes, and many more like them, that medal hangs on the wall with their many others or is stuffed away in a trunk. Many of their friends and business acquaintances do not even know they were athletes, let alone that they won gold medals in the Olympics.

That is not to say that winning in the Olympics doesn't or didn't mean a tremendous amount to them. I think you would be hard-pressed to find an Olympic champion who did not assign some special private meaning to winning that Gold. For many U.S. amateur athletes, however, reaching the apex of their sports has little impact on their subsequent careers or personal lives. The Bruce Jenners, Mark Spitzes, and Jim Craigs are rare. For most amateur athletes the hard, tangible rewards are few, if any. The private satisfaction is often great. Equally often, however, is a hard realization that what appeared so special and important is nice, but doesn't shake the world.

These considerations coupled with the powerful odds against your reaching these kinds of heights make it important for you to weigh the extent of your investment with the likely or even possible returns. Reach for the stars—there are real rewards to be had. And even if you do not get there, the trip is often worth it. But get a good idea of what is waiting for you at the end of the road. Then decide if it is likely to be worth the trip. You don't want to reach your goals after years of long and hard training only to discover it's no big deal. That can be devastating.

Have I Outlined a Likely Road to Success?

The world of sports offers no guarantees. All you can do is give it your best shot. But make sure you are traveling on the right road.

Many people who want to lose weight struggle through all sorts of weird, expensive, and torturous diets. Yet they avoid exercise like the plague. Just the thought of pushups, situps, or running sends them scurrying for the refrigerator. These people have it all wrong. Surprise! Pushups and situps do little for weight control. And running is no better than walking.

You lose weight one way and one way only: by consuming fewer calories than you burn up. Pushups and situps contribute a little to cardiovascular conditioning and help extensively with increased strength and muscle tone, but you burn up very few calories with these exercises. Walking burns just about as many calories as running, if you cover the same distance.

Make sure you are traveling the best route. Doing the right thing is much more important than doing things right. It is possible that practicing your putting might help you rush for 1000 yards this year in football, but it is highly unlikely. Surely you can be impacting your skills more directly.

It would be super to set your sights on making the Olympics by placing among the top four finishers at the Olympic trials and to finish fourth. But to do that, only to find out that only the top three finishers make the team, could blow you away.

Check the facts and carefully scrutinize your plans. You want your short-term goals and strategies to give you the best chance possible of realizing your long-term objectives.

How Much Control Do I Have Over Reaching My Goals?

Try to set your goals such that you can exert as much control over the outcome as possible. To a very large extent, this means setting behavioral goals, instead of goals for the outcome of the competition.

You have a great deal of control over what you do in a race; you have less control over how you place in that race. No matter how fast you run, someone else may run faster.

Sports like tennis make it even more difficult to control the outcome. You can place the ball exactly where you want it and your opponent may still make a diving save that hits the top of the net and trickles over, falling out of reach for a winner. In team sports like football, it is even more difficult for an individual to control the outcome. Take 22 men, a slippery field, and a ball that bounces unpredictably and throw in a few imperfect officials— and who knows what can happen? In baseball, you may hit .374, belt 56 home runs, drive in 157 runs, and win a Golden Glove award, and your team still might never make it to the World Series.

You do, however, have control over what you do. And you can set your goals accordingly. Even where training is completely structured by a coach, you can set goals for your performance within that structure.

It is easy for you as a competitive swimmer, say, just to go through the motions of daily practices set up by your coach. In fact, earlier I gave the example of setting goals for doing hypoxic training, sprinting, pulling with paddles and tube, weight training, dry land exercises, interval training, or long slow distance in order to increase speed, strength, and endurance. In most cases, the coach would be the one that would go through a careful analysis, determining the specific drills to be used in each practice session. As a result, unless you do some extra on your own, or provide some input to your coach (which rarely is a bad idea), you have little control over the structure of your training. And you probably will not even be told what the training routine will be until the time to do each drill.

Nevertheless, you still ultimately have responsibility for what you get out of training. Get the most out of each practice by setting goals for things you know you can do no matter what the drills.

For instance, you may want to lead your lane at least a certain number of times each week, or be sure to use full range of motion on at least a specified percentage of repetitions on weight training. You can always decide to set goals for each drill as you learn what is to be done. For instance, strive to make a certain interval or breathing pattern, or set a goal to get past the second line on your pushoffs before you start your stroke.

No matter what your sport, before each practice session or preferably prior to each individual drill, ask yourself what I call Keith's question (you can call it by your own name): "What can I do to get the most out of this opportunity?" Then convert the answer to action!

Take control. It is up to you to do it. No one else is going to be able to do it all for you, even if they wanted to. Let your goals reflect this fact.

What Opportunities Exist?

The Olympics only come once every four years. That is worth remembering. Strive to make the Olympic team and win yourself some Gold, but also set some other goals for yourself. If you put all your eggs in one basket (especially one that occurs infrequently and has tremendous odds against success), it will be more difficult to stay motivated. And if you miss that rare opportunity, a tremendous amount of work can all seem to be for nothing.

Similarly, you very well might identify some likely means of reaching the goals you seek, but be lacking the financial resources to avail yourself of the opportunity. If this is the case, don't give up. Restructure your goals. You may have to ride the bus instead of flying first-class, if you get my drift.

Time and physical capabilities should also be considered. Deficiencies in these areas might very well warrant new or modified goals.

Are There Other Ways of Reaching My Goals?

Many youngsters think that sports can be their ticket out of the ghetto or pay for their college education. They see that many professional athletes are earning exorbitant salaries and huge cash prizes. There are $100,000 challenge matches in tennis, $50,000 first prizes in golf, and multimillion-dollar contracts in baseball, basketball, football, and hockey. A few superbly skilled athletes find gold at the end of the rainbow, but many, many more never get hold of the pot.

The Reverend Jessie Jackson has been imploring black youngsters to put their time and energy into studying to become lawyers, engineers, physicians, and the like. The odds of making it are much greater. Athletic scholarships can pay for college, but they are hard to come by. They also can be lost quickly with injuries or poor performances. Scholarships also are often accompanied by subtle or blatant messages to put sports above studies, even if it means not graduating. Some coaches and schools demonstrate ample concern for their student-athletes. Others care little if the student graduates after he has used up his eligibility.

If nothing else, athletic scholarships soon may be a thing of the past, especially for the so-called minor sports. Economic pressures, federal legislation, and changing priorities may lead to need-only financial aid to education.

The youngster who aspires to an athletic scholarship to college or a professional career in sports does well to examine alternate means of obtaining the same rewards. If a swimmer spent as much time delivering newspapers or in some other paying job as he did training and competing, he could pay for at least some of his college education. That is a relatively sure thing. An athletic scholarship is tremendously uncertain. The Little Leaguer eyeing the big leagues is like the purchaser of a sweepstake ticket, except the Little Leaguer invests so much more. There could be a super payoff if he wins, but there are some small returns and many more losing tickets.

Sports return a variety of precious rewards to active participants. Examine what is in it for you. See if there might be easier, more cost-effective ways of getting what you want. You may choose to take an alternate route to your goals. You may not. You will, however, be clearer about what you are doing and why.

SETTING PRIORITIES

There is no way you can focus your attention and efforts at once on all of the training, game or meet, and career goals you have established for yourself. You will have to establish some priorities and trim down to a few goals to work on at a time.

Listing your long-term goals in order of importance to you is a good place to start prioritizing your goals. Then list the short-term goals that you have established for each of your long-term goals and rank-order them consistently with the first list. This will give you a very basic list of immediate objectives in order of their long-term importance. This list, however, warrants further attention. You will want to narrow it down to a few goals to set your sights on each week.

Some of the short-term goals you have generated will facilitate realization of more than one of your long-term objectives. Similarly, one goal might automatically be achieved by achieving another. For example, I swim almost every day. In order to control my weight, I find I do well to swim at any pace at least 4000 yards at least three days per week and at least 2000 yards at least two other days. I also like to compete in Masters swimming meets. In order to be prepared to compete at a level I find enjoyable, I think I do well to swim at least 6000 yards two days per week and at least 4000 yards at least two other days. For the purpose of training for competition, cardiovascular conditioning, and good muscle tone (appearance) I am more concerned with effortful responding than I am for the purpose of weight control. Whenever possible, I try to train with a competitive swimming team in order to insure a challenging practice complete with good competition. Well, if I train with a team and meet my goal of at least swimming a hard 6000 yards two days per week and 4000 three other days, I need not attend at all to my goals for weight control. They will automatically be accomplished through realization of my goals for training for Masters competition.

Some of your goals may not require any purposeful attention. Although they may be important to achieving your long-term objectives, it makes little sense to give high priority to that which you accomplish out of habit.

Some of your goals may be in conflict with each other. For example, raising your individual statistics may not be consistent with adherence to team goals. Similarly, many coaches have had to struggle with a conflict between their goals of instilling certain values in the athletes in their charge and coaching winning techniques, while many student-athletes are torn between the conflicting demands of sports and academics.

Prioritizing your goals can be a difficult task. Nonetheless, it can put things in clearer perspective. The recreational tennis player I spoke of earlier who was sacrificing his relaxation and recreation to his "competitive spirit" does well to remember that winning is nice, but other goals are much more important for him. On the other hand, if you are participating in sports to keep in shape or for social reasons, you might want to consider what additional gains you might realize from some increased effort. As long as you are putting in the time, why not put in some more effort and give it all you have got to win?

Of course, your priorities will change as your interests and proficiencies change. Thus it is important to periodically assess your goals and reset them as necessary.

Keeping your goals flexible, however, does not mean changing short-term goals in response to momentary whims that may either obscure the larger picture or fail to take it into account. Your short-term goals should be consistent with your long-range aspirations.

CONCLUSION

Goal setting can be a complex and often confusing endeavor. There are many issues involved. Goals can take many different forms. And they can be set across a day or a lifetime.

When set correctly and employed properly, goals can be tremendously useful tools. They can be motivational, inspirational, and behavior-directing.

Your goals should cover the full range from your long-term objectives, and the reasons for wanting to reach these heights, to the daily behaviors that will facilitate realization of your long-term goals. You should set goals for weekly training, meets or games, the season, and your sports career. Your goals should be clearly specified as measurable standards of behavior to be performed. They should reflect a plan built to program-in a fairly steady progression of success experiences. At the same time, they should help you reach for high standards that encourage more fruitful outcomes. Finally, your goals should be flexible, so that you can change them as appropriate.

PART TWO

THE CHALLENGES

5

MOTIVATION

It's not the best man that wins, it's the best trained man.[1]

RUNNER WALT STACK

The road to athletic success is hard and full of obstacles. At the higher levels of competition it takes conscientious practice merely to maintain skill and conditioning and even more devoted practice to improve. Sometimes it seems too much. You can get tired of practice, too focused on the unpleasant aspects of training, doubtful of the value of your goals, questioning of your commitment, or disheartened by your lack of progress. Then motivation wanes.

In this chapter, I will outline some practical strategies for motivating your training and competitive performances. First, however, it is necessary to understand two very basic motivational concepts: expectancy and incentive value. Expectancy and incentive value are integral to generating the interest and enthusiasm that supports persistent, intense, and sustained performance. Motivation comes with greater incentive and increased expectancy of success.

EXPECTANCY

Expectancy is the anticipation that under a set of circumstances a particular behavior would lead to a particular outcome. Expectancy regarding the outcome of your behavior in a given situation is a major determinant of behavior. You approach goals or engage in activities that you *expect* to have desirable outcomes and you avoid activities that you *expect* to have unpleasant or aversive outcomes.

90

There are three component beliefs that affect expectancy: (1) you must believe a certain action has a strong causal connection to a particular outcome; (2) you must think that you have the ability to perform that action; and (3) you must trust that your action will likely result in the specified outcome. Only then is the expectancy of success high.

Unless you believe a particular behavior will help you achieve your goals, you will not be motivated to do it. It would not make much sense to practice painting landscapes in order to refine your field goal kicking skills. Nor would you be motivated to shine your shoes so that you could pitch better. Similarly, motivation to train declines when you fail to see how today's practice will affect the outcome of next month's game. You must see the meaningfulness of what you are doing.

It is also crucial that you believe you have the capability of reaching your goals through diligent effort. Confidence is critical to motivation. If you do not believe you have the talent to make it, you are not likely even to try. Diligent training or effortful performances may not be expected to compensate for this lack of talent. Then if you do not think you are going to make it anyway, why make an effort? Where is the motivation? The "untalented athlete" might be taught to persist and work hard as his only possible avenue to success. But he still needs to believe that he has enough talent, or capability, to overcome the odds through his efforts. If he believes he doesn't have it, the expectancy of failure will diminish motivation.

The expectancy of success increases the motivation to perform, and higher expectancies generate greater motivation. The odds are important. You need to expect that success is likely. Motivation depends on how much you expect that your efforts will pay off and how valuable that payoff is. No matter how potentially great the incentives, if you think you are unlikely to attain those rewards, there is little or no motivation to perform. Tug McGraw's appeal to his 1973 New York Met teammates that "Ya gotta believe!" reflected the fact that increased expectancies heighten motivation.

INCENTIVE VALUE

Of course, expectancies alone do not strengthen motivation. There still must be some incentive value in the anticipated outcome. For example, you may know that if you enter a local race you are almost certain to win a blue ribbon, but if you have no interest in winning that ribbon, and that particular victory would have no meaning to you, you may not ever enter that race, let alone vigorously pursue victory. Marathoner Bill Rodgers suggests that winning is partially dependent upon "what the race means to you." He says, "That often affects how hard you run the race. Maybe the difference between winning and second."[2]

The more incentive value the expected results have, the more motivating they are. Greater prospective payoffs are more motivating. You can increase incentive value by increasing the amount, quality, and proximity of reward.

Usually larger amounts of potential reward provide greater incentive. A big trophy usually elicits more motivated performances than does a small one. Similarly, larger purses are more motivating than smaller amounts of prize money.

The context within which the amounts are perceived also impacts incentive motivation. Probably because of this, in recent years many professional athletes making hundreds of thousands of dollars per year have sought to renegotiate their contracts. Presumably these huge amounts were attractive when they signed. But when other players started getting substantially larger sums, or these players began performing as well as others in higher salary ranges, their contracts apparently seemed less attractive.

The quality of reward is another factor affecting motivational strength. The more preferred a reward is, the greater incentive value it provides. An Olympic Gold Medal provides much more incentive than does a gold medal of equal size and physical attractiveness from a local meet. A victory in a traditional rivalry means more than one in a less intense rivalry. While in either case a victory is only one win, the meaning associated with each win alters the incentive value of the victory.

Incentive motivation also is stronger the closer you are to your goal. Thus, a football player frequently gives it a little extra when in a defensive player's grasp with the first-down marker inches away than he might if he had 20 yards to go. That same football player would probably drive even harder inches from the goal line where the rewards are not only closer but more valuable. Likewise, the last lap of a race, or even the last repeat of an interval training series, usually produces more effortful performance.

Similarly, if there is too long a delay between your actions and their payoff, it is difficult to stay motivated. It is hard to get interested in doing something that only might have some payoff months later, especially if that something has some unpleasant aspects. That is one of the most difficult parts of getting motivated to practice. If you can keep rewards more immediate, you can facilitate motivation.

MOTIVATION FOR TRAINING

It is unfortunate that most discussions of motivation center around the conditions which best elicit good performances in the meet or game situation. Motivating yourself to perform well in the competitive event is certainly of the utmost importance. In most instances, however, motivating yourself to train hard regularly is by far the more formidable challenge.

You do things that you expect to be rewarding (or rewarded) and avoid doing things that you expect to find unpleasant. Most things, however, are neither purely attractive nor purely undesirable, but have elements of both. This is especially true of athletic training. Depending on the particular sport, training can be immediately tedious, fatiguing, boring, and/or painful, while many of the built-in incentives are uncertain and far off in time. Motivation will reflect a balance of the many long- and short-term aversive and desirable aspects of any given situation. But you can tip the scales toward the strong motivation to train by intentionally providing yourself with incentives to train and by increasing the expectancies that training will pay off.

Training and Expectancy

If you see little or no relationship between training hard and performing well, you will not be likely to train consistently hard no matter how much you desire to do well in competition. Unfortunately, far too many athletes believe that top game or meet performance requires superlative concentration, motivation, and effort at the meet or game, but only moderate preparation. They seem to believe that as long as they are in decent shape, basically know what to do, and are naturally talented, then if they are sufficiently "up" for the game or meet and give it all they've got, they will perform as well as they can. These athletes honestly do not believe that by preparing better, they can significantly improve their performances. Instead, they expect that a moderate amount of training and a good "psych" yield the best performances.

While most mature athletes have little doubt that their practice behaviors have some influence on subsequent meet or game performance, many athletes do not see a strong relationship between their performances in training and those in the athletic event—and with good reason. It quickly becomes obvious to all neophyte athletes that there is not a one-to-one correlation between performance on any given drill, any day's practice, or even an entire season's training and subsequent performances. Nor is it always the athlete who works the hardest who does the best.

Especially if an athlete began participation in sports at an early age, the other factors that influence athletic performance may seem much more important than diligent training. In the younger age groups, athletes notice that physical maturation largely determines levels of performance. It is amazing how much time youngsters who aspire to athletic excellence spend thinking about growing and sitting around waiting to grow, rather than training. The expectancy is that physical development will produce the desired outcome. Skill development may be expected to help some. But many athletes do not develop the belief that persistence and effort in training will pay off in the long run.

Since the development of rudimentary sports skills often comes easy and yields large performance returns, many talented athletes fail to learn the relationship between practice and improvement. As a result, when they reach a level of competition that requires an extraordinary commitment of time and effort to training in order to reap the minimal improvements that separate the field, they frequently fall short. It is not that they do not care or are lacking in motivation, "desire," or "determination." They simply do not have the expectancy that training hard will produce good performances. They fail to realize that the refinement of the skills that they learned so easily produce only diminishing returns and that these smaller gains are harder-earned.

Furthermore, differences in performances that accompany different intensities of training often are not noticeable. When they are, you frequently discover that you perform better (in the short run) when you do not train as much or as hard. You often do better with rest. That is why, for example, swimmers taper the amount of their training just before meets. But you cannot rest too frequently and still build the strength and conditioning that come with consistent, hard training. Balancing the short-term performance benefits of rest with the long-term benefits of intense training can be a difficult task. Getting a good, clear understanding of the relationship between effort in practice and performance gains can be harder still.

I firmly believe that, although many breakthroughs in levels of performance occur in games or meets, the majority of breakthroughs occur either in practice or as a result of the foundation laid in training. A moderate amount of conditioning and strength building and a basic understanding and adequate proficiency of the skills involved are poor substitutes for the strength, speed, endurance, and automaticity of response that come from conscientious, hard training.

Increase Expectancy

One way to increase your motivation to train is to acquire better understanding of the reasons for your training activities. This is especially important if you do not find training fun. The less enjoyable you think your training activities are, the more important it is that you understand their importance and their contingent relationship to your goal achievement. You must perceive practice as meaningful. Then you will be much more motivated to train.

If you train with a team, presumably your coach has a pretty good idea of what he is attempting to accomplish in practice sessions and has formulated a training plan specifically designed to accomplish those goals. Usually this planning revolves around knowledge about principles for developing the ingredients of successful performance stemming from studies of exercise physiology, kinesiology, biomechanics, and the strategies and philosophies of the particular sport. All too often, however, coaches do not share with their athletes the basis from which they plan practices. Instead, they demonstrate the "do it without question" approach that has historically characterized coaching of sports in the United States.

Fortunately, more and more coaches are educating their athletes, and increasingly more athletes are taking it upon themselves to learn about the principles behind optimizing human performance. This is critically important to motivation. You have to believe that your training activities will lead to good performances and that the best performances stem from conscientiously striving to improve with each and every practice drill, or motivation for training will suffer. Dianne Holum, speed skater Eric Heiden's coach, says Eric "believes in his training." As a result, she says, "Eric does everything as hard as he possibly can."[3]

If your coach has allowed you to participate in setting goals and designing a training program that will best enable you to reach those goals, you will have a better understanding of what you are trying to accomplish in practice and why. If he has not, ask him to discuss this design with you or the whole team.

All too often, coaches understand the importance and principles of training so well that they just naturally assume that their athletes also understand them. But often athletes do not. As a result, differences in practice performances are not always indicative of motivation. You may fail to train consistently well, not because you do not care or are lacking in motivation, but rather because you do not have the expectancy that working certain drills (or practice in general) will produce good performance in the game or meet. Then when you fail to put out in practice your coach mistakenly assumes you do not care, you are lazy, or you lack desire—or he just gets angry from the frustration of watching you waste an important opportunity. (Remember, he knows it is important and may assume you do.) You may even question whether you care, when really you just do not understand the relationship between what you are doing and where you are going, or you doubt your ability to get there regardless of how hard you train.

If you train without a coach, you have probably been forced to understand the relationship between practice and performance in order to design your own training program. Many people, however, merely take suggestions or copy others' seemingly successful training strategies in making up their own training program. If this is the case, you should back up and reconstruct the basis for this design. Building a pyramid to success that has specific training activities as its foundation (as suggested in Chapter 4 on goal setting) fosters motivation for training. Understanding why you are doing what you do in training and how that will lead to improvement will help keep you motivated to train.

Similarly, you need to understand that, although each individual practice activity or even each individual practice session by itself may not affect performance in the long run, collectively they will. One loafed drill or one missed practice probably will not matter. For that matter, dogging or missing any drill or practice session all season long will probably not make any difference in the long run. But they add up. And they add up fast. One missed practice probably will not matter. But two might. And one becomes two—and two leads to more. Moreover, loafing or skipping practice tends to become a habit. Each time you dog a drill, go through the motions, or skip it entirely, you practice that approach. Then the next time a similar situation arises you are more likely to do the same, until finally you begin to dawdle, casually approach drills, or forego them unthinkingly.

Think of training as a jar full of unpopped popcorn where each kernel represents one of the year's practice drills, an entire practice, or a related activity relevant to your goals (a good meal or a good night's sleep, for instance). A full jar of popcorn gives your best chance of reaching your long-term goals. If you remove only one kernel it will probably make no noticeable difference in the level of popcorn in the jar. And it does not matter which one you take out. Take any one out. Put it back. And take out any other. The level remains the same. No matter which one you take out, the level does not perceptively differ. If ypu take one out and leave it out, however, removing additional kernels makes more of a difference. As you remove more and more kernels, the level diminishes. Still, each time you remove one it is difficult to notice any difference. But as they add up the difference clearly shows.

It is the same with training. It is often difficult to see how any one drill or practice matters. And probably it really does not matter that much by itself. But collectively they do. And they add up quickly. Especially in this day when the margin of victory is often not a matter of inches or seconds, but of millimeters and thousandths of a second, you may not want to take a chance on hurting your chances of success even the slightest bit.

So the next time you are faced with the decision whether or not to work a drill, how hard to work it, or to go or not to go to practice, just think "Popcorn!" to yourself. You will know what it means. As distance runner Craig Virgin says, "There should be a purpose to every single work-out you do. You're not out there to waste time."[4]

THOUGHTS AND EXPECTANCY

MOTIVATIONAL SELF-TALK   Your thoughts will play a large role in promoting or inhibiting motivation to train by increasing or decreasing expectancy. Thinking that will motivate good training performances will include reminders of the contingent relationship between training activities and their probable consequence, reminders of the long-term benefits of resisting temptation, and convincing predictions of good performance.

The Relationship Between Your Actions and Their Probable Consequences.   Sooner or later you are going to question why you are training (or at least why you are training that day). Then it helps to know why. By frequently reminding yourself of the relationship between what you are doing and the expected outcomes, you promote motivation for your training. Old adages such as "practice makes perfect" (which, incidentally, might better be stated: "practice of perfect performance makes perfect") are reflective of these kinds of reminders. Other examples include:

> "This will help me build strength."
> "I've got to stay with it if I want to make the interval."
> "The more I do this, the more automatic it will become."
> "Concentrate! It'll pay off."
> "Making all eleven practices this week will help me get to the Nationals."
> "These wind sprints will help me in the late innings."
> "Popcorn!"

The Long-Term Benefits of Resisting Temptation.   It's difficult to opt for the tedium or pain of training when alternatives are easier. Similarly, there are many temptations that are tough to pass up. Peer pressure makes it even more difficult. But others often don't share your goals. You can keep yourself on track by reminding yourself where you are going and how these temptations can interfere with your getting there. Examples include:

> "I'd like to go to the party, but I'd rather get some sleep and stay healthy."
> "One drink once in a while probably won't hurt. But one often leads to two and two to twelve. And once in a while leads to all the time. Besides 'probably won't hurt' isn't good enough—I want every edge I can get on my competitors."
> "I don't want to go to morning practice. I'd rather sleep. . . . But, that won't help me make cutoffs."
> "Popcorn!"

Predictions of Good Performances.   It is a lot easier to get yourself to do something (especially if it has some aversive aspects) if you not only think it will be worth your while, but feel confident that you can succeed. Self-statements predicting good performances foster that confidence (see Chapter 6). Examples include:

> "I'm going to smoke this workout."
> "You can handle anything coach can throw at you."
> "I've got it!"

"I can hit this 'turkey.'"
"This one's going in."

COUPLE MOTIVATIONAL SELF-TALK WITH SELF-INSTRUC-
TIONS   Talking to yourself in this manner sets the stage for
motivated action by fostering positive expectancy. Goal-directed
behavior can be further facilitated by intentionally pairing this type of
motivational self-talk with self-instructions. For example, "This will
help me build strength" can be immediately followed by "Stay with
it!" or "Pick it up!" "I don't want to go to morning practice. I'd rather
sleep ... but that won't help me make cuts" can be paired with "Get up
and get to practice!" and "I'm going to smoke this workout" can be
coupled with self-instructions to "Get after it!"

REDIRECT NEGATIVE THINKING   From time to time your
thoughts will tend to inhibit motivation by decreasing expectancy.
You have to learn to recognize these self-statements that interfere
with motivation and get yourself back on track by using countering,
relabeling, and self-instructions. Examples of thinking that tends
to deter motivation for training include statements questioning
the value of training and predictions of poor performances.

Statements That Question the Value of Training. It is often difficult to see the collective effects of many individual activities
or the relationship between what you do now and how well you
will do later. But when you question the value of training, most
often you are really making the statement that there is little or no
value in what you are doing, not merely looking for the true value.
The following are examples of this type of motivation-inhibiting
thinking (possible implicit messages are in parentheses):

> "Why am I doing this?" ("This won't help!" Or "This can't possibly
> do me any good." Or "I'm not ever going to make it anyway!")
> "I don't need this!"
> "Why am I here?" ("I should not be here." "This isn't doing me any
> good." "I can't benefit from this.")

You can refocus your attention and direct your actions more
appropriately merely by substituting self-instructional thinking,
such as "Get after it," "Remember your goals and work for them,"
"Do it right!" or "Get the most out of practice. Concentrate!"

Or you may have to restructure this type of thinking so that your thoughts more readily elicit more goal-directed training responses. Countering techniques work well in these instances.

For example, you could counter "Why am I doing this?" with thoughts like "Because I want to get in shape," "This will help me build strength," or "You know darn well why you are doing this. You want to make it. If you are going to be there when it counts, you've got to pay your dues. If you're willing to practice and do it right, you've got a chance of making it. Do it!"

You could counter negative thoughts like "I don't need this!" with statements like "Who says?" "What makes me think this isn't going to help me?" or more in-depth counters like "Maybe you don't need this, but how can you be sure? Anyway, it won't hurt you to get after it even if you are uncertain as to its relevance to your particular situation. Besides, what if it is important? And as long as you are out here you might as well get as much out of it as you can. If nothing else, you are building good training habits that will pay off in your approach to other training activities!"

Similarly, "Why am I here?" can be handled with thoughts like "Because you want to make _____ [Nationals, the Olympics, the pros, the team, your goals, etc.]" or more in-depth counters like "Where's the evidence that I shouldn't be doing this? I want to do it when I remember my long-term goals. Every practice and my approach to it might make the critical difference for me."

Often you can control for the detrimental effects of thoughts that question the value of training by merely relabeling your training activities as desirable or important. Thoughts like "This is important," "I really want to be here," or "This is helping me" provide a more motivating perspective.

Predictions of Poor Performance.   Anytime you do not think you can handle a training activity or you think you will do it poorly, you are less likely to be motivated to get after it or to do it at all. Thoughts reflecting these beliefs only tend to reaffirm these opinions, making them stronger and interfering with motivation. Examples of such negative thinking are as follows:

> "You can't do this, turkey."
> "I'm no good at this."
> "I can't make this interval."

It is important not to let this kind of thinking stand. Turn it around with countering. Remember, this kind of thinking is problematic. It interferes with motivation. As a result, it is easily countered. The evidence is on your side. If nothing else, it is not useful because it decreases expectancy, thereby lowering motivation.

"You can't do this, turkey" is easily countered with thoughts like:

> "Who says?"
>
> "So what if I've never done it before. There's no reason to believe I can't this time. There has to be a first time. Anyway, this kind of thinking won't help me. Think more positively."
>
> "Calling yourself a turkey doesn't help. It only creates the expectation that you are incapable, lazy, or undeserving and will fail. That's a bunch of garbage. Get after it."

Similar counters can be employed to manage other predictions of poor performances.

Of course, championship thinking will better promote motivation for training if it is coupled with action. The more evidence you can muster through education to demonstrate that your training activities will benefit performance, the more believable your intentionally produced self-motivating thinking will be. The more success you build in by setting progressively more desirable but readily attainable short-term goals, the more convincing your predictions of good performances will be. And the more your thoughts are followed by conscientious, effortful training performances, the more you will continue to produce expectancy-increasing self-motivating thoughts.

Training and Incentive

While there is usually plenty of incentive available to motivate meet, tournament, or game performance, the same often is not true for the practice situation. In fact, most of the incentive to train lies in the relationship between practice and performance in the competitive situation. It is largely the expectancy that training will pay off somewhere down the road that motivates you to train. That payoff, however, remains built into performance in the sports event and not into training. There is little or no payoff delivered contingent upon good practice performance. Even worse is the fact that training is often aversive. Athletic competition has

become so intense that athletes must engage in long hours of arduous work, give up attractive competing activities, and delay a host
of immediate pleasures that might otherwise be available in order
to have a chance at success. Practice can be boring, tiring, painful,
and can conflict with other attractive or otherwise important
pursuits.

Since the incentives to train are not there, you need to provide them for yourself. The more you can make practices interesting and rewarding, the more you provide yourself with the motivation to train. To the extent that training can be made interesting,
exciting, fun, or intrinsically rewarding, motivation is not a problem. When training is not rewarding in itself, however, it can
indeed become a problem.

Motivation to act comes from incentive. It is the anticipation
of an activity being rewarding or rewarded that elicits action. In
general, incentive motivation is greatest when it is anticipated
that rewards will be delivered contingently (when, and only
when, your goal is met), consistently, and with minimal delay. If
an action is not fun or has no payoff, then it will occur less often.
If the payoffs for the hard work you put in during practice are
delayed or uncertain, then it is difficult to maintain the motivation
needed to train diligently. Yet this is precisely the situation in
sports: Most of the rewards for hard work in practices come from
the much-delayed and iffy rewards that accompany good meet or
game performances. The longer the delay and the less certain the
expectancy of that training paying off, the lower the motivation
to train.

If there is too long a delay between practice sessions and any
payoff, then it is easy to question the value of training (especially
when you are bored, hurting, tired, cold, or hot and sweaty). As
a result, you often may have difficulty seeing how working a particular drill will affect your chances of making the Olympics,
which may be two years away; or how exerting yourself on a
preseason conditioning exercise will affect your team's chances
of winning the championship game.

The longer the delay between performance and its payoff,
the greater the incentive required to keep you motivated. People
do train long and hard in an attempt to reach their goal of making
the pros or the Olympics four, six, or even eight years away. And
some of these people do it with little apparent payoff along the
way. (I say "little apparent payoff" because I think this kind of

"self-motivation" is almost always accompanied by self-talk prais-
ing good training performances and cueing anticipation of future
reward.) Nothing else seems to matter. But this solidarity of purpose is rare. And when it does occur and the individual fails to
reach his goal, it can be devastating. Often, even if the goal is
achieved, the reward may be disappointing (not potent enough to
make all those years of training worthwhile). It seems to be as
Gertrude Stein once said of Oakland: "When you get there, there
isn't any there." Marathon world record holder Alberto Salazar
speaks of seeing "these guys like Coe and Ovett you'd thought
were superhuman, and then you get a world record, and they're
just a couple of guys. We're just people, we just run a little faster.
It's kind of depressing, really, when you think about it."[5] Many
athletes do go into deep depressions after winning a major sporting event, largely for this reason. Similarly, many others "hang it
up," feeling that even the payoff of reaching the pinnacle of their
sport does not make it worth doing it again.

If the payoffs only come when you reach your goals for that
one big game and not for meeting training goals or goals for games
of lesser importance, then that one performance situation (the
Olympic trials, for example) can become too vital. The lack of
payoff for training has made the anticipation of reward in this one
situation too precious. Getting the reward seems to be necessary
(rather than desirable), and the prospect of not getting it becomes
awful (rather than disappointing at the opportunity lost), subsequently engendering performance-debilitating anxiety (see
Chapter 8). Then if you cannot overcome the detrimental effects
of anxiety to achieve your goals, there is no payoff at all accruing
from all the hard work and time spent in preparation. Instead,
self-abnegation is likely to occur, suppressing motivation, lowering confidence, and further minimizing the chances of future goal
achievement.

On the other hand, if you can make training fun or provide
yourself with regular hard-earned rewards for training activities
until they do produce natural, rewarding consequences (such as
satisfaction or coach or peer approval), then no matter what the
long-term payoff, the trip has been worthwhile. Getting there can
be half the fun.

If you are involved in a lifetime activity like jogging or swimming for your health, you never "get there." Then it is essential
that the "getting there" is enjoyable. Or you very well may stop.

Increase Incentive

Build in as much enjoyment as possible. The more intrinsically rewarding practice is, the more you will be motivated to train.

VARY YOUR TRAINING

Variety helps. Doing the same thing over and over can be a drag. The more you can vary your training, the more enjoyable it can be.

MAKE A GAME OUT OF IT

Of course, repetition is often necessary in building and over-learning skills. If you or your coach approach training creatively, however, you can make it more fun. Games and contests can turn boring drills into exciting activities. They also carry built-in rewards.

Many coaches use scrimmages not only to simulate the game situation, but also to make conditioning exercises more enjoyable. Others make repetitious or painful conditioning drills more interesting by building goals or competition into the exercise. Notice how hard two players train when their workouts have become a contest to decide a place on the team.

You may be surprised to find that if you view each activity creatively, you can make some kind of game out of it. Mike Bruner, the 1976 Olympic 200-meter butterfly champion and world record holder, frequently endeavored to make the practice of race techniques and strategy into games. When pushing off the walls in practice he would try to keep up with a teammate for as long as possible without swimming in an attempt to develop "super walls" for his races. Similarly, he often would pick the nearest teammate at the end of a repeat and simulate a race situation where he would try to "touch-out" (touch the finish before) his opponent.

Even if you cannot arrange to make your training activities into contests, you can always employ your imagination, as Mike Bruner did, to create competition. You can get awfully careless practicing your layups by yourself. But if you bring Moses Malone out to guard you, you have to work that much harder to get to the basket. Similarly, every run can be the Boston Marathon. And every play can be fourth and goal in the Super Bowl.

FIND INSPIRATION IN MODELS

Many athletes find inspiration in watching others perform in high-level competitions. There is nothing like watching the championships to get you interested in playing in them. This is an excellent strategy for evoking interest. Unfortunately, its effects on motivation for training are usually short-lived. A strategy with longer-lasting effects may be to use a prestigious source as a training model. Thus, instead of going to see Greg Lemond, Steffi Graf, Tom Kite, Wayne Gretsky, or Michael Jordan play, go watch these top athletes train. It takes diligent practice to achieve their level of skill, strength, and stamina. Let them inspire your training by example.

TRAIN IN A PLEASANT ENVIRONMENT

The context in which you train can make it dreary or fun. A run around an indoor track in an old building may not do as much for you as a run along a lake. Better lighting, new equipment, a smiling companion, and some good music can all enhance your motivation to train.

VIEW PRACTICE AS FUN

The only real difference between work and play is the way you look at it. Merely relabeling practice drills as fun, exhilarating, challenging, or invigorating, instead of viewing them as dull, boring, tedious, or a necessary evil, can intensify motivation. Relabeling can be especially effective if you use these new labels to get yourself looking for the fun, exhilaration, challenge, and invigoration in practice drills. Perspective makes a tremendous difference.

APPRECIATE USING YOUR BODY

Exercise usually feels good. Of course, when fatigue and boredom set in as a result of effort and repetition, the good feelings can get overshadowed. Make a point of appreciating how good it feels to use your body. That is a large part of what makes sports rewarding.

SET GOALS FOR TRAINING

To the extent that practices are intrinsically rewarding you will be more interested in getting there and staying involved. The opportunity to engage in fun activities with people who have common interests in a pleasant, stimulating environment can serve as powerful incentive motivation. For some recreational athletes, this is what sports are all about. For the competitive athlete, however, this is not enough. You do not want practice just to be fun, you want to make enjoyable and rewarding the practice activities that will lead to performance excellence in competition. You want to make it fun to train well.

Setting goals for training is probably the most effective way of providing yourself with incentives for conscientious, hard training. Training goals help you to bridge the gap between practice activities and their rewards. They give you something more immediate to shoot for and make your daily practice more relevant. Instead of (only maybe) getting rewarded for training at some far-off time (if you perform well in competition), you can have a clear criterion from which to intentionally reward daily performances.

If you have good training habits, they will clearly show up when measured against your training goals, evoking the feeling of accomplishment that will help maintain motivation to train. They will also help you to see the areas that need improvement.

REWARD YOURSELF
FOR A JOB WELL DONE

If you need to develop better training habits, more immediate payoffs are essential. Especially if training is not rewarding in itself, you have to reward yourself for training. Training goals will provide you with the structure within which to provide yourself with some incentive for training diligently. That incentive can be set up by arranging it so that you get some payoff for reaching training goals. Anticipation of that payoff will motivate behavior. In other words, set it up so that you receive a reward for attainment of training goals.

The feelings of accomplishment stemming from training well (and knowing what long-term rewards that will reap) can be, and often are, reward enough. Athletes are known to work long hours each day for years without receiving many evident rewards. (Again I say "evident rewards" because more than likely there are congratulatory self-statements acting to maintain this "self-motivated" behavior.) It is this kind of "self-motivation" that is applauded. And people do persist in responding for some time, seemingly without reward. This would seem to be adaptive. The chances of succeeding are increased considerably if you keep try-ing even without reward. But training hard need not be reward enough. Nor is it in any way more noble to train hard in the absence of obvious immediate rewards than it is to get some imme-diate payoff for your efforts. Furthermore, rewarding yourself to train makes good sense, because it works.

Some rewards are necessary to establish good training habits and to maintain them (especially since there are aversive aspects of training). Without some payoff, boredom, disinterest, and even depression can result. Frequent reward, on the other hand, builds and maintains an interest in what you are doing. And anticipation of reward "gets you up."

Intentionally set it up so that you will reward yourself for a job well done. Anticipation of that reward will provide the incen-tive for producing the practice behaviors that will get you to your training goals.

Even if your athletic interests are more casual or purely recre-ational, the motivation to train may involve similar issues. If you jog regularly, for example, mainly to stay in shape, maintain your weight, and perhaps increase your resistance to coronary disease, you face the same motivational problem. Many of the returns for jogging are delayed in coming (conditioning, increased muscle tone) and some are far off and iffy (increased longevity), while many of the displeasures are immediate and more certain (pain, fatigue, boredom, the time not available for other pursuits). Simi-larly, even if you are a casual tennis player, you are sometimes called upon to play when you would prefer another activity (you need to keep your weekly game intact). You may want to engage in conditioning work or engage in the laborious repetition of par-ticular shots in order to enjoy your game more because you per-form more proficiently. If you do want to reach your goals, you will want to be certain to provide yourself with incentives that will keep you on track. Besides, it's much more fun that way.

USE REWARDING SELF-TALK   The most powerful rewards you can adopt will be self-rewarding thoughts. This rewarding self-talk often will be automatically accompanied by a warm, good feeling. This is probably a large part of what - constitutes the feelings of accomplishment derived from training hard of which I spoke earlier. The difference is that you can intentionally think these self-rewarding thoughts contingent upon reaching your goals for training. Thus, after you have set the goals, attainments that match or exceed your goals can be used as cues for making positive evaluative self-statements. Following performance at or above standard, say things to yourself such as "Way to go!" "That's the way to work!" "All right!" "I did it!" "I was smoking!" "Good!" "That was a great set!" or "You got it!" The feelings of accomplishment that follow may not seem as natural at first. Nevertheless, it effectively gets you tuned in to the importance and pleasure of training well and gets you motivated to do so again.

It is unfortunate that our society does not encourage us to pat ourselves on the back when we do well. This kind of self-reward maintains good training behavior. And it feels good. Congratulatory self-statements are effective.

Of course, overt self-congratulation may be met with accusations of bragging. But you can think to yourself how well you did, and you will benefit from doing so.

ENLIST THE AID OF OTHERS   Covert payoffs work extremely well. But there is nothing wrong with arranging to receive praise from others or even material rewards for a job well done. These rewards can effectively provide incentive motivation.

Attention, praise, recognition, social acceptance, or even a smile from people important to you can be contracted for as a reward for good practice performances.

Some people are reluctant to arrange for these (or other) kinds of rewards, thinking that if they contract for them, they won't mean as much. That's possible, but only if you decide to discount their worth. You need not do that. And you may be surprised how spontaneous a smile or praise can be, even when prearranged, especially if it is made contingent upon reaching a goal that the other person knows is important to you.

UTILIZE TOKENS, ACTIVITIES, AND MATERIAL REWARDS   If you belong to a team, your coach may reward good game or meet performances with gold stars, buckeyes, or other stickers to be attached to a football helmet. These token payoffs provide incentive for superlative game performance. Players work hard to get them. The same principle can be applied to practice performance. You can reward attainment of your day-to-day practice goals by treating yourself to a new piece of equipment, some clothing, that book you wanted, some candy, ice cream, or your favorite meal (high-caloric rewards will obviously not be the payoff of choice if you are trying to keep your weight down!). Or you can give yourself money, points, coupons, or the like which can be saved and later exchanged for other types of rewards. (If you do this, it helps to display a graph of your progress toward accumulating enough money to purchase your reward.)

Movies, games, conversation, bubble baths, long showers, whirlpools, picnics, time to relax, watching sporting events, reading a good book, and many, many more enjoyable activities can be made contingent upon reaching your practice goals. Anything that can provide some added incentive or that by being associated with training activities makes them more enjoyable is worth arranging.

SELECT INCENTIVES THAT ARE BARELY ATTRACTIVE ENOUGH   Of course, you don't want to provide yourself with exceedingly potent rewards so frequently that reaching your practice goals becomes so rewarding as to supersede the value of achieving your long-term goals. If you did, it would be difficult for the rewards accruing from attainment of your long-term goals to maintain their incentive value. Then you might lose your motivation to win the big ones. Making getting there half the fun would be nice (and really ought to facilitate getting there). But keep it half the fun. Don't make it all the fun.

The key is to "dangle a carrot" in front of yourself that is just barely attractive enough to maintain motivation for reaching progressively more desirable goals (ones gradually closer to your long-term objectives). It doesn't make sense to celebrate reaching a practice goal, such as practicing your serve today until you have gotten at least 100 in, in the same way you would celebrate winning the NCAA championships, the U.S. Open, or Wimbledon. If you did, winning Wimbledon would probably hold no more attraction to you than would getting 100 practice serves in the service course. Yet you do want to reward yourself for reaching your training goals. So you might treat yourself to an ice cream, a movie, a T-shirt, or a pat on the back for reaching your training goal, while you might treat yourself to a two-week vacation or an evening on the town for winning the big one. The trick is to be pleased and encouraged with your progress so you'll keep at it, but not to get overly ecstatic about small gains (though some small gains, particularly if you have seemingly leveled off, will be cause for celebration).

It is an art that may take some practice to develop. But it is important that you do so. Usually your best estimate of what rewards are barely powerful enough to provide you with enough incentive to train (the way you feel you need to in order to maximize your chances of getting where you want to go) will be your best bet.

Develop Self-motivation

When you are first developing good training habits you get best results if payoffs come immediately and every time. Once learned, good training habits can be strengthened by gradually decreasing the frequency with which they are rewarded (psychologists call this thinning the schedule of reinforcement). In fact, irregular and intermittent rewards produce the most persistent, sustained responding. Over time, you can reward good training performances less often and with more subtle rewards (satisfaction, for example) while still providing incentive for persistent practice behaviors. In this way, you can develop "self-motivated" training habits.

KEEP YOUR LONG-TERM GOALS
CLOSE AT HAND

By providing yourself with rewards for training well, you effectively increase the incentive to train. Another way to increase incentive for training is to bring the incentive value of your long-term rewards for training closer in time to the behaviors necessary to reap those rewards. Of course, you cannot actually do this. But you can keep them close at hand symbolically by intentionally thinking in a manner that will facilitate motivation to train.

Based on prior experience, observation of others, instructions, and self-talk you learn to anticipate the consequences of your actions. This anticipation can influence your behavior and enable you to endure long waits between performances and payoff. Indeed, in most instances, you are motivated by and work for anticipated payoffs rather than immediately rewarding outcomes.

It is anticipation that brings the delayed consequences closer to the behavior in question. If you have set up your own incentive system, you can predict with reasonable confidence what the consequences of your actions will be. Thus, you know you will reward yourself if you do a good job in practice. Secure in this knowledge, and with a small cognitive sampling of the impending reward, you can withstand greater delays in delivery of rewards and still have the incentive to work hard.

You can foster the anticipation of reward by intentionally focusing on and talking to yourself about the consequences of your actions and the contingent relationship between those behaviors and their resulting rewards. In this way, you bridge the temporal gap between what you are doing and the rewards to be realized at a later date, thereby promoting incentive motivation.

Thoughts that help increase incentive include reminders of the long-term benefits of conscientious, hard training and statements stressing the importance of your actions and the value of their consequences.

REMIND YOURSELF OF THE LONG-TERM BENEFITS OF CON-SCIENTIOUS, HARD TRAINING   By reminding yourself of the benefits of what you are doing in training, you provide yourself with more incentive to do it and do it well. This is especially helpful if the immediate drill is aversive (painful, fatiguing, boring, or in some other way unpleasant).

General statements about the benefits of training can be helpful. Of particular utility, however, are those ideas that reflect the gains to be derived from the specific drill being engaged in or about to be performed. Examples of these kinds of thoughts follow:

> "OK, my arm hurts, but that's how you build strength."
> "This drill is boring. But it will help me do it right automatically in the game, when I don't have time to think."
> "OK, I'm exhausted. But this is building endurance."
> "This is going to help me get to the big leagues."

STRESS THE IMPORTANCE OF YOUR ACTIONS AND THE VALUE OF THEIR CONSEQUENCES   Reminders of the contingent relationship between your actions and their probable consequences and predictions of good performances promote positive expectancies. As previously mentioned, expectancy alone is not sufficient to motivate performance. You still need incentive to act. By stressing the value or importance of your actions and their consequences, you provide yourself with that incentive. Examples include:

> "You're doing this because you *want* to win the Nationals."
> "This drill is going to help build strength and endurance." (Said in such a way as to indicate the personal importance of strength and endurance)
> "I'm here because I want to be. I want to do whatever it takes to . . . [make the pros, make the Olympics, win the regionals, etc.]."

REDIRECT NEGATIVE THINKING

Of course, your thoughts can also act to decrease the incentive to train. Thinking that draws your attention to the aversive aspects of training, that devalues the consequences of training or the training activities themselves, or that reminds you of the importance of or attractive aspects of alternative activities interferes with incentive motivation.

COUNTER THOUGHTS DEPICTING TRAINING AS AVERSIVE

Most training sessions are neither purely attractive nor completely aversive. Some parts of practice are fun. Other parts seem less enjoyable. The more you draw attention to the unpleasant aspects, the less incentive you have to train. Thinking about the aversive components seems to make them weigh more in importance, tipping the scales toward avoidance behaviors. Exaggerated labeling of the aversive side makes it even worse. Common examples of this kind of thinking are:

> "This is boring!"
> "I'm tired."
> "My arms hurt!"
> "Time sure flies when you're having fun!" (Said facetiously)

Countering your thoughts and relabeling your activities less pejoratively will help you get back on track. Statements like "This is boring!" can be countered with thoughts like "It is—if you decide it is. It need not be. Look for the fun parts. If you can't find any, make it fun!"

"I'm tired!" could be handled with a "So what?" or even a facetious "Poor baby!" either of which implies it's not that terrible.

A sarcastic "Time sure flies when you're having fun!" can be handled with "Who says you always have to be entertained. . . ."

You're here because you want to be, because you want to reach your goals. This is important and will help. . . . It's not useful to focus on not enjoying it . . . it only gets you down and keeps you from remembering why you're here. (Notice that, when countering, you can always refer to the uselessness of your dysfunctional thinking. If your thinking is interfering with your goals, it is easy to argue it down.) Think about your purpose and get going! It's worth it."

COUNTER THOUGHTS THAT DEVALUE TRAIN-ING Thoughts that discount the value of the rewards you are likely to reap from training necessarily lessen the incentive to train. These thoughts differ from the above-mentioned statements questioning the value of training, though the wording may be identical, in that they imply that the rewards are not worthwhile; while the aforementioned statements questioning the value of training imply that the training will not lead to reward. Examples include:

> "Who cares?"*
> "I hate this!"
> "What's so great about . . . [tennis, swimming, football, a pro career, making the Olympics, etc.] anyway?"
> "What am I doing here?" (Implying: "I don't like this.")

"Who cares?" for example, might be countered with a simple "I do!" Or "I hate this!" might be reproached with a reminder that it is easy to think that way when you are physically tired, but that it is the fatigue speaking, not your usual sentiment.

Thoughts like "What's so great about this sport anyway?" or "What am I doing here?" are more easily countered if you know where you are going and what you want out of the trip and/or reaching the destination. (See Chapter 4.) Reminding yourself of your motives provides incentive.

COUNTER THOUGHTS THAT PLACE HIGHER VALUE ON OTHER ACTIVITIES When the going gets tough or tedious it's tempting to remind yourself of other more pleasant things you could be doing. All that serves to do is get in the

---

*Notice that it is the disguised message ("I don't care") in rhetorical questions that must be countered.

way of what you are doing. It is senseless to keep trying to escape something you have already decided to do. Yet we all interfere with the quality of our training from time to time with statements like:

"I could be home asleep!"
"I need to be studying!"
"I could be home snuggling with my girlfriend/boyfriend!"
"Everyone else is watching the football game!"

When thoughts like these rear their ugly heads, talk to yourself more sensibly. Employ counters like:

"But you're not! So concentrate on what you're doing."
"Yes, you have studying that needs to be done, but now is not the time or place. You can do something about that after practice. Right now do a good job of what you are doing."
"Yeah! I could and that would be nice. But it won't help me reach my goals. This will!"
"Everyone else doesn't have your goals!"

Championship thinking is an important part of maintaining and increasing the incentive to train. Championship thinking can help keep the rewards psychologically close to the activities. Without these psychological prompts it can be difficult to "get up" for some of the lesser games, let alone to get motivated for every drill in each of your daily practices.

Thoughts of your long-term goals will often keep you working hard. Sometimes anticipation of far-off, uncertain rewards will not work. But this anticipation, coupled with the incentive provided by attractive rewards to be delivered more immediately, can better keep you working, while making training more fun. Provide yourself with the needed incentive to train consistently hard with your thinking skills and by intentionally rewarding yourself for reaching your training goals. Quite simply, getting rewarded for practice performance can make practice more rewarding.

MOTIVATION
FOR THE CONTEST

Most of the time motivation for the contest is not a problem. This is what you train for. The incentive is there because the rewards are there for the taking. And you anticipate having fun, knowing that athletic competition is stimulating, exciting, and exhilarating.

There are times, however, when you have trouble getting "up" for a contest. Usually this occurs when you are relatively indifferent as to the outcome, you expect to win easily, you expect to do poorly, you are fearful of the outcome (or the contest itself), or some combination of these factors.

If you are indifferent as to the outcome, you may find yourself halfheartedly going through the motions. No matter how capable you are, you will not do well (or perform at all) if you do not want to. Even Superman probably would not win a race, hit a homer, or gain as much as one yard off tackle if he did not want to. Unless there are relatively attractive incentives available, you just do not get after it. Incentives are necessary to motivate performance.

It is relatively rare when you find yourself lacking motivation for the big game or meet. Some of the less important events, however, may lack the excitement and rewards that engender incentive motivation. This seems to be partially a hazard of experience. The more opportunity you have to vie for the big ones, the less exciting and rewarding the lesser events may tend to be. This also may be a problem of volume. The more you participate, the harder it is to see that the outcome of that one event has long-term importance. Major league relief pitcher Kent Tekulve echoed this idea when he said that "the toughest problem in baseball is to keep yourself pumped for 162 games a year."[6]

If you expect to win easily, overconfidence can impede motivation. Why try, if you will win no matter how well you perform? Attack this kind of complacency with reminders of the value and importance of good performances. Remind yourself that competitions, no matter how sure is victory, provide great opportunities for preparation for more tightly contested events. Remind yourself of the kind of habits you want to build. And remind yourself that victory may not be as easy as it seems. It may come easy with concerted effort, but may slip away with lackadaisical performance.

If you expect to do poorly, you are setting yourself up for failure. Poor expectancies about the outcome inhibit motivation. You must anticipate some payoff for your efforts if you are to have any incentive to perform.

Expectancy of poor performance can lead to disinterest. It often is difficult to give it your all in the face of what appears to be certain failure, especially if you inappropriately think that if you try and fail you will be a failure (see Chapter 8). Why try, if you are going to fail anyway?

Furthermore, anticipation of nonreward often yields depression or lethargy. This kind of thinking and these emotional reactions can deter good performances.

If you are fearful of the outcome or of the event itself, then competition can be aversive: These unpleasant aspects of the event can generate avoidance motivation, shifting the balance of positive and negative incentive. Even if you like to participate and are attracted by the possible payoffs, if you are afraid to lose, to hurt, or to confront your opponents, motivation is dampened.

All too often there is some combination of these factors. When faced with tough competition many people overestimate the likelihood of failure. They become afraid of that prospect or depressed when faced with it. And they try to protect themselves against the perceived aversive consequences of the presumed forthcoming poor performance by feigning or actually generating disinterest.

In any case, the strategies for motivating good training performance in the athletic contest are the same as for motivating good performance. You get yourself motivated by providing greater incentive and increasing the expectancy of reward.

Increase Incentive

The incentives are usually there for the contests. Often, however, you overlook many of the rewarding aspects of the competitive experience. As a result, you may find it hard to get "up" for a game. When this happens, remind yourself of the importance of the upcoming event, the value of the event, and the value of the rewards you are likely to reap from doing well.

By intentionally focusing your thinking on the rewarding aspects of the competition, you increase the incentive to perform. Remind yourself of the rewards already structured in the event. Emphasize the collective importance of individual events in the standings. Tell yourself that the upcoming event can mean adding one victory to the win column and that that will take you one step closer to the championship. Think about the medal, trophy, or cash prize you can obtain by performing well. (Notice that it is important not only to focus on the attractive awards and rewards associated with the event, but to think about them as resulting from performance. You want to motivate yourself to *perform* well, not daydream about getting goodies!)

Remind yourself of the excitement of the competition—the exhilaration that comes with completely engaging yourself in meeting the challenge.

Look at the event as an opportunity to reach a goal you have for yourself, a chance to go after a personal record. And remind yourself of the team goals for the competition and how you can contribute to them.

Even if you do not have any goals for the particular event, a little thought can enable you to generate some incentive. Suggest to yourself that as long as you are going to do it anyway, why not set some goals for yourself, get into it, and strive to do it well. If nothing else, by really getting engaged in what you are doing, you are much more likely to enjoy the process.

Approach the competition as an opportunity to strive for excellence. Remind yourself how good you felt last time you did well. Tell yourself you can feel that way again by putting it all together in the same way.

Think about the recognition that can come from performing well. Media coverage, the opportunity to perform in front of friends or family, a hometown crowd—all may be motivating for you.

You may be able to stimulate your interest by deciding to put on a good show for the crowd. Or you might view the contest as an opportunity to promote your sport.

Stress to yourself the importance of good performance. Even if the outcome does not seem important, the habits you build are. Lesser competitions in many ways are your best chance to practice for major competitions. They often closely simulate the experience you will have in the big meet.

Stressing the importance of the competition is one of the things that many of the better coaches do best. The proverbial locker room pep talks "fire the teams up" by bringing some symbolic meaning to the contest, thereby increasing both the value of the victory and incentive motivation. You may not be able to "win one for the Gipper," but you can find your own causes to rally around. You even may want to dedicate a game performance to a particular practice drill or even to "Popcorn."

Intentionally decide to value the event itself and the rewards available for good performances. Actually tell yourself, "This is important." Think things like "This is a good opportunity to use what I've been practicing." Focus on the nice things about the awards and elaborate on their attractiveness. You might think thoughts like "That trophy is nice. I'd sure like to have it. It'd look good sitting on my bookcase."

If you still have difficulty generating interest in the event, provide yourself with some incentive by selecting a reward for yourself to be received contingent upon achieving some goal. The goal and the anticipated reward can bring some added purpose to your efforts in the competition. It doesn't have to be natural or spontaneous; it just has to work!

Be careful not to make the outcome of the event too precious. If it becomes too precious, you tend to focus on thoughts like "What if I do poorly?" or "What if I blow this rare opportunity?" Then the event can become scary. You get anxious and distracted. You are focused on what you do not want to happen instead of what you want to do (in this way imaginally practicing the wrong behaviors). As a result, you are more likely to choke and perform poorly. Strive to perform well and to achieve victory, not to avoid failure and defeat.

Increase Expectancy

The myths and misconceptions like those that frequently interfere with motivation for training do not seem to be paramount forces in inhibiting motivation to compete well in the contest. A little bit of the feeling that "I can do it when it counts, even if I don't do it here and now" occasionally slips into some athletes' approaches to the lesser contest, but rarely in the big game.

Far and away the major factor inhibiting motivation for the major competitive events, however, is a lack of confidence. If you have little or no expectancy of success, there is little or no motivation to make a strong, concerted effort. Assuming the incentive is there (which it usually is for major events), motivation increases with belief in relatively high chance of success. In Chapter 6 I will discuss confidence and suggest ways to increase this expectancy.

6
CONFIDENCE

A very strange thing happened. Even though I didn't give myself much of a chance against Connors, when the newspaper reporters and everyone asked me what was going to happen (if it came down to Connors and me in the final) I had to tell them that, of course, I thought I was going to win. So they started asking me why, and I started to think up reasons. And the more I thought about reasons . . . the more I began to realize that I really was going to win. And when I finally went out on the court, I was very confident.[1]

RAUL RAMIREZ (following his victory over Jimmy Connors in the 1978 American zone Davis Cup finals)

Did you ever have the experience of standing over a putt and knowing that it was going to go in, then knock it in, just as you knew you would? Or maybe you knew you were going to double-fault and, sure enough, you did.

Then there were those times when you were less certain about how you would perform. Sometimes you surprised yourself. But most of the time, the more confident you were of victory, the more often you won. The less confident you felt, the less often you came through.

Confidence is critically important to performance. It tends to act as a self-fulfilling prophecy. If you do not believe in your ability to perform well or the probability that you will, you probably will fall short of your goal. Whereas if you think you can do well, you are more likely to come through. But there is nothing magical about the effects of confidence. Rather, a look at the characteristics of confidence readily points to how it impacts performance.

CHARACTERISTICS OF CONFIDENCE

Confidence is characterized by a high expectancy of success. It involves thoughts and images reflecting the beliefs that you have the capacity to perform the actions required for success, that there is a high probability that you will exhibit these behaviors, and that there is a high probability that success will result from these actions. In other words, when you feel confident, you know you can do it, you predict you will do it, and you predict that doing it will lead to success.

These high levels of expectancy naturally interact with motivation. If you think you will win, you are more likely to try. And as long as expectancies remain high, persistence in the face of adverse circumstances remains high. You are not easily dissuaded by temporary setbacks. On the other hand, if you think you cannot win, you have less motivation to exert any effort or even to participate. Why try, if you are going to fail anyway? There just is no incentive.

Similarly, your expectations shape your goals, which in turn play a significant role in determining your behavior. Confidence allows you to reach for the stars, while a low expectancy of success limits the level of aspiration that guides and directs your actions.

Confidence arouses positive emotions. The exhilaration, exuberance, and joy that accompany confidence in the performance situation frees you up for loose, strong, quick, and fluid execution. Moreover, when you are confident, you are more likely to remain calm and relaxed when faced with the performance situation. On the other hand, impaired confidence engenders anxiety, leaves you with a vague feeling of apprehension, and depresses your mood, all of which tightens you up, distracts you, and inhibits good performance.

Confidence gets you moving toward success instead of trying to avoid failure. When confident, you tend to focus your thoughts and images on coping with the environment and your opponent, on mastering the task and on the rewards that will accrue from success, rather than worrying and catastrophizing about performing below par and the consequences of doing poorly. As a result, you are mentally rehearsing successful action, rather than imaginally practicing (and thereby programming in) poor performances.

Furthermore, confidence facilitates focused attention on the task at hand. The focus on trying to avoid failure that comes with a lack of confidence tends to impair concentration. It makes you more easily distracted and deters you from your purpose. You tend to worry about how you look, how well you are doing, or how things are going to turn out rather than concentrating on what you are doing.

Confidence further reflects some very basic assumptions about your role in the competition. A confident approach is an assertive approach, one that respects your right to compete and to win. Too often, a lack of confidence is indicative of a belief that you are not deserving or worthy of victory, or even a place in the competition. Deficient confidence even may arise from a fear of offending others by outperforming them. These basic assumptions may impair your inclination to try and constrict what efforts you do exert.

There is nothing magical about the effects of confidence. The resulting performance levels are logical extensions of the motivation, concentration, and specific actions that evolve from the thoughts, images, and beliefs that characteristically make up confidence.

Nor is confidence something that either you have or you do not. You can build confidence through work and planning. You can practice capturing it. And you can learn to evoke it at will.

BUILDING CONFIDENCE

The Blueprints for Building Confidence

A history of success experiences breeds in an expectancy of future success. The more often you succeed, the more you expect to succeed. These expectations may take the form of explicit predictions of success or a general feeling that you can succeed. In either case, this confidence is partially built through experience. Therefore, to the extent that you can arrange for a high percentage of success experience, you can build confidence.

A fairly steady progression of success experiences is aided by setting realistic goals that are readily attainable with persistent, conscientious, effortful action. In this way, you draw the blueprints for building confidence.

Just as properly set goals will make it easy for you to succeed relatively consistently, perfectionistic goals set you up for failure and impair confidence. There is no way you can reach perfectionistic standards. This you know. You can hardly be confident of doing something you know cannot be done.

There is nothing wrong with having high aspirations and striving for perfection. That is how great performances are achieved. The problem arises when perfection becomes expected (in the sense of being demanded, not predicted) and becomes the sole criterion for measuring success. It is reasonable to expect that because you did something once, you are therefore capable of doing it again. But too many athletes mistakenly believe that because they do something once, they therefore *should* do it that well, or better, every single time. Demanding that you should be successful implies that there is something wrong with you if you do not succeed. Then, when you inevitably have some failure experiences, you naturally begin to wonder if there is something wrong with you. These failures are evidence that maybe you are not capable after all, or at least no longer capable.

Avoid perfectionistic goals. They only set you up for failure. And avoid demanding that you *should* achieve success. Rather, confidently predict that you will succeed.

The Foundation for Confidence

There is no surer way to feel confident than to be thoroughly prepared. You build strength, speed, flexibility, technical skills, strategy, and automaticity of response through rigorous training and practice. Jack Nicklaus knows this. He says, "As long as I'm prepared, I always expect to win."[2] Runner Brendan Foster looks at it from the other side. As he puts it, "You can't be confident without doing the training."[3]

Nothing elicits confidence like already having experienced what you are setting out to do. Part of your preparation should include this rehearsal. You are likely to have little doubt about your capability of achieving your goal if you have already matched that level of performance in practice. The more often you have done it before, the more confident you will be of matching or bettering that level of excellence. It even is easy to feel confident of breaking the world record if you have already done it in practice. Thus, if you want to run a 3:48 mile, there is no better way of gaining confidence in your ability to do it in a meet than to have already done it in practice. Even repeating a series of 56-second quarters with little rest would enhance your confidence. Similarly, if you can handle the veer, consistently turn a double play, or long jump 27 feet in practice, it will be easy for you to feel confident of doing the same in competition.

Of course, it is not easy to break a world record in practice, to win Nationals for the first time, to beat an opponent you have never beaten before, or to win a championship you have never won before. Some of these things you never have the opportunity to achieve prior to the competitive situation. But you can always preplay a success experience. Imaginally doing the thing before bolsters confidence.

Imaginally practice successful performances prior to your competition. Experience what it is like to give the winning performance. (Put the emphasis on "give the winning performance." Experience and practice the action!) And know what it is like to have won. The satisfaction, the attention, the rewards—all are worth getting familiar with. Make winning a reality. Get to know it. (At least make it a real possibility, not something that is so unfamiliar that you cannot even imagine it.) The unknown can be scary and difficult to be confident of achieving.

Familiarity breeds confidence. Acclimate yourself to the conditions under which you are going to perform. If possible, visit the site of your event in advance. Learn where everything is. Visualize what it will be like to be there amid the hustle and bustle of the crowd and the other competitors.

If you cannot visit the site in advance, try to view films, videotapes, or still pictures of similar competitions at that site, or at least pictures of the setting. Play sound recordings of previous competitions. Descriptions of what it is like are also helpful. Use all this information to set the stage for imaginal practice. Preplay your winning performances within the context in which they are to take place.

And know your opponent. In team sports, or sports like tennis or fencing, where your opponent can affect your performance, this is crucial. Game films, scouting reports, and so on are invaluable. Knowing your opponent's strengths, weaknesses, typical strategies, and so forth not only direct your preparation and game plan, but stimulate confidence. Of course, your performance in sports like swimming, golf, gymnastics, track and field, and diving can be unaffected by your opponent's performances. Nevertheless, some familiarity with their preevent antics can help keep you from getting distracted or psyched out, helping you to maintain confidence.

Practice Feeling Confident

Most of us tend to think of confidence as a state or feeling that we either have or we do not. We tend to look at it as something that seems to happen to us. In fact, most of the time we let nature take its course. If we feel confident, great! If we do not, we get concerned. But it need not be that way. Confidence is a state of mind that you can intentionally evoke. With practice you get better at calling it forth at will. And you can build habits that will have you automatically feeling confident when faced with competitive situations.

Begin by imaginally replaying successful performances. Reexperience the feelings that accompanied previous successes. Recapture that winning feeling. Get to know these feelings. They are yours. You create them. And the more familiar they are to you, the easier it is for you to evoke them at will.

If they are available, watch films, videotapes, recorded radio descriptions, or still pictures of your previous good performance. Otherwise, amass them for future use. In 1980, the year George Brett gave .400 a good chase, he attributed breaking out of an early season slump with a three-for-five, four-RBI night to viewing a video cassette of the 1978 playoff game against the Yankees where he had hit three home runs and came within a couple of feet of two more. "I did this for a couple of hours yesterday. Not only can I see how I was swinging the bat when I was doing it right, but I'll tell you, this is a hell of a confidence builder too."[4]

You even may want to tape-record a description of what it was like immediately after a successful experience. This way, you can describe the event, and how you feel, while the meaning is still fresh and you still are experiencing the winning feeling. This will provide you with a vivid, detailed description to be played later.

As you review your performances, relive the feelings that you felt when these events took place. Notice how easily you recapture those feelings with minimal prompts. Make note of the fact that you recreated that feeling. Reexperiencing these feelings in this way is evidence of how easily you can intentionally call up confidence and a winning feeling and is good practice for doing so.

Think Confidently

Confidence largely consists of thinking you can do it, you will do it, and you will have success doing it. Intentionally think this way in performance situations. And practice thinking in this confident manner. The more you practice thinking confidently, the more automatically performance situations will elicit thoughts, general feelings of confidence, and resulting positive action. As marathoner Bill Rodgers says, "If I think I can win, ho, am I tough."[5]

AFFIRMATIONS:
THINK THAT YOU CAN DO IT

Affirm your capacity and tendencies to reach your goals. Frequent affirmations will help you to maintain confidence in your ability to get the job done. If you have doubts, affirmations will get you to consider your potential. They will raise the possibility and probability of increased capacity.

Remind yourself of the things you do well. List areas of potential. Of course, you cannot measure ability or potential, just performance. Nevertheless, you can always do better. If nothing else, it is useful to approach performances with that mind set. As long as you do a good job of goal setting (programming for a fairly steady series of success experiences without limiting the level of aspiration or predicted performance) and of evaluating your performances, it helps to believe you can always do better. Pittsburgh Steeler Jack Ham says, "I actually think I need to feel that . . . I can always improve."[6] This belief sets the stage for directing action that will lead to better performances.

Thoughts like "I adjust well to unexpected events," "I make things happen," "I like to give that little bit extra," "I enjoy a challenge," "I come back strong," "I frequently make the big plays," "I can do it," "I can hit anyone," "I work hard in practice," "I perform well under pressure," and "I play aggressively" encourage a postive approach to athletics and a confident feeling about yourself and your capabilities. If worded well, these affirmations will establish an open-door policy for superlative performances.

Too often athletes limit their performances in advance by decisions, beliefs, images, or general feelings about what they are capable of doing. Labels such as "sprinter," "lazy," "choker," "early bloomer," and "slow starter," can be particularly detrimental by defining and limiting the possible range of performance. Yet even if there are real physiological limitations to your level of performance (which, though they exist, we presently have no way of identifying), it is not useful to approach your performances from that mind set. It is much better to believe you can do so much more.

Of course, complimentary labels are better than derogatory labels. Disparaging labels lower the expectancy of success and lead to a lack of confidence. Flattering labels often boost confidence. Obviously, this has some advantages over labeling that impairs confidence. Nevertheless, there are some potential problems even with complimentary labels. Most salient of these is the

126

danger of overconfidence. Overconfidence and a lack of confidence both can hamper performance through a lack of action. While this lack of action stems from a defeatist belief when you lack confidence and stems from a complacent attitude when you are overconfident, in both cases performance suffers from the belief that whatever you do will not affect the outcome. A lack of confidence is characterized by high predictions of failure *independent of actions*. Overconfidence is characterized by high predictions of success *independent of actions*. Either way, the belief is that whatever you do really does not matter. Confidence, on the other hand, is characterized by high predictions of success *based on performance*. When you are confident, you are motivated to act; knowing your actions will determine your level of success. Labels often tend to make you think that it is something about you (some quality you have—or lack) that will lead to success or failure, rather than attributing the results to your actions.

Labels also imply a permanency that often gets challenged by the facts of your experience. Thus, even if you label yourself positively and bolster confidence, that confidence can be impaired when your labels are brought into question by temporary setbacks.

You do much better to avoid "I am _____" in your affirmations. Instead, emphasize the action. Action-oriented affirmations like "I do _____" and "I like to do _____" are more useful than passive affirmations. The difference is small, but the resulting subtle effects can be profound. Affirm the capabilities and potential with positive, action-oriented self-statements about what you do and can do.

Take further care with the wording of affirmations by avoiding perfectionistic statements such as "I always _____" or "I never _____." These often are impossible to live up to.

Keep your affirmations in the present tense. The purpose of affirmations is to build up your confidence in what you are capable of doing now. Reminders of past successes and predictions of future successful performances have their place and also are important. They, are, however, distinct from affirmations.

THINK THAT YOU WILL DO IT
Affirmations can be too general to suffice alone. They do not specify when and how you are going to do well. They merely point out your tendencies and capacities for doing well. Like the positive thinking ("Day by day, in every way, I am getting better

and better") proposed by the French psychotherapist Émile Coué, affirmations are not sensitive to situational conditions. That does not mean they are not effective. They are. They help boost confidence. But you also should raise confidence with thoughts that specify situationally specific action.

Knowing you can perform well is not enough. You still need to believe you will perform well. Think of the specific acts you *will* perform in order to succeed in this situation. Tell yourself things like "I'm going to exploit my opponent's weakness," "I'm going to do a job on my opponent's backhand," or "I'm going to cover my man like a hand with a glove." Emphasize the odds of your successfully performing these behaviors. Predict with great certainty that it will happen. And emphasize the action, not the results. If you perform as desired, the results will take care of themselves.

This kind of thinking helps elicit the desired action. Practice—and use it. Of course, the more this thinking is accompanied by and followed with appropriate action, the more believable it becomes and the more likely you are to continue to think in this confident way. This adds up to a beneficial circular reaction. Thus, when you tell yourself you are going "to take the lead early and build it" and subsequently take the early lead, it becomes easier to confidently think you are going to extend your lead and to even more confidently go about doing so.

REMIND YOURSELF
OF YOUR PREPARATION
AND YOUR PREVIOUS SUCCESSES

Affirmations of your abilities and predictions of successful performance are most believable when supported by the evidence. So muster up all the evidence you can. Remind yourself of all the things you did to prepare for the upcoming performance. And remind yourself of previous successes.

Even if you have not prepared perfectly (which no one ever does), now is not the time to remind yourself of the imperfections in your training activities. There is a lot of room for imperfection. You need not train perfectly to be strong, fast, flexible, well conditioned, skilled, and well practiced in plays, strategies, and timing. Of course, the more prepared you are, the better. But given where you are at any given time, it behooves you to focus on the things you did to prepare and how well you did them.

Similarly, you need not have a history of succeeding every single time in order to believe you are going to succeed this time.

In fact, you need not ever have succeeded before.* You can still do well now. Whatever successes you have had, however, are worth focusing on. They gain more weight as you attend to them and act as good evidence for your predictions of forthcoming successful performance. And of course, while reminding yourself of what you did well in the past, you tend to practice those good performances and recapture the feelings that accompanied them.

Reminding yourself of the preparation you did and of your previous successes can help you feel confident of doing well in upcoming events. Frequent reminders of preparation and previous successes will help build a general tendency to approach things more confidently.

Counter Thinking
That Impairs Confidence

From time to time even the greatest athletes have doubts. You will, too. But you need not give much credence to these thoughts. When they occur, don't pay any attention to them. If they persist, counter them and redirect your thinking.

Just like the rest of us, Jimmy Connors has days when things seem to be stacked against him. But he pays little attention to his doubts. Here are some of his thoughts on confidence:

> The whole thing is never to get negative about yourself. Sure, it's possible that the other guy you're playing is tough, and that he may have beaten you the last time you played, and, okay, maybe you haven't been playing that well yourself. But the minute you start thinking about these things, you're dead. I go out to every match convinced that I'm going to win. That is all there is to it.[7]

Thoughts that reflect doubts about your ability to perform well or about the likelihood of your good performances leading to success impede a confident approach to competition and impair motivation. These kinds of thinking should be recognized and immediately countered.

Most often these thoughts take the form of "I can't win," "I don't know if I can beat Joe," "I probably won't be able to hit this guy," "I probably won't win." "I don't have it today," or the like.

Attack this kind of thinking with thoughts like "I can too!" "Where is the evidence that I can't?" "What makes me think I

---

*If you had infrequent or no previous successes, this may be a good time to emphasize heavily your capability and your preparation.

can't win?" "That's correct! I don't know if I can beat Joe. I'll find out. In the meantime, I'll have a better chance of beating him if I approach it with confidence," or "It's not doing me any good to think I probably won't be able to hit this guy. Whether I will or won't remains to be seen. It will be easier to hit him if I tell myself I can (and believe it) and focus on doing it rather than on probably not being able to."

Catch your doubts, counter them, and plug in confident feelings and thoughts. Remember, confidence is not something that needs to happen to you. You get yourself feeling and thinking confidently or fail to do so. You can make it easier to counter doubts and plug in confidence by practicing similar scenarios and using situations, as they come up, as opportunities to utilize your psychological skills.

Discarding Your Self-Rating System: The Foundation for Asserting Yourself

We tend to act as if we are deserving, nondeserving, worthwhile, or worthless human beings. As a result, some athletes ensure defeat in advance of the competition by not believing they deserve to win, have the right to win, or are good enough people to win. Others hinder success by believing they ought to win, whether or not they put forth the effort, merely because they are good people.

It is very natural to look at yourself in this way: as good, bad, deserving, undeserving, worthwhile, or worthless. Natural, but neither correct nor useful.

It is natural to look at yourself in these ways because that is the way other people look at you, the way they act toward you, and the way you are taught to see yourself. From the time you are an infant, people respond to you in terms of your worth to them and how your actions compare to their values and the standards they have for you or people in general. Their responses imply or explicitly tell you that you are "good" or "bad." Through their actions and words, parents, teachers, coaches, friends, and other people significant to you let you know what they like and do not like about your behavior, appearance, abilities, and your Self (your very worth as a person).

Others impact how you feel about yourself through their evaluative statements, attention, and behavior. When you do something appropriate or at high standards, people tend to say "what a good boy" or "what a good girl." When you do something inappropriate or poorly you tend to hear "What a bad boy!" or

"What a bad girl!" Teachers and coaches may identify you as a good model or poor model for others. They may label you. And they may treat you as worthwhile, competent, and attractive, or as worthless, incapable, and undesirable. You may be sought out, fawned over, ignored, or ostracized by others. All this and much more influence your developing feelings about yourself.

Of course, ultimately, you are responsible for how you feel about yourself. You interpret others' behavior, you internalize others' negative and positive evaluations of your performance and your self. You choose to believe and incorporate others' opinions or to reject and ignore them. When others compliment or criticize you or your behavior, you have many choices. A "That was good" might be heard as "I am good" or as "That was good for someone as incompetent as I am," or rejected with a "No, it wasn't" or "Thanks, but it really stunk." A "You play terribly," could be taken to mean "I'm no good" or "I play terribly," or rejected with a "What does he know?" You filter out, interpret, and evaluate the messages you get from others.

Similarly, you are the one that models other peoples' behavior and learns to evaluate your Self. Only you can decide "I'm no good at that" or "I'm bad."

The development of these feelings about yourself is natural. It is learned. But you are responsible for maintaining these dysfunctional behaviors and outlooks. And you can change. You can free yourself up to approach your performances confidently and assertively by discarding feelings and assessments of your worth. If you accept yourself as you are and do not try to rate or measure your Self, you will approach performance situations more confidently, more assertively, and with less fear and apprehension. It is much more useful and makes more sense.

The process begins with the manner in which you evaluate your performances. There is great value in evaluating your performances, when done properly. Assess the level of your performance so that you can celebrate a job well done. Enjoy your success. Dwell on your successes. Give them enough attention and weigh them enough in importance so as to expect to succeed again.

Note what you did well. And compliment and reward yourself for doing so. That way you will be more likely to repeat those acts.

Assess where your performances fell short. Notice inappropriate or inadequate responses. Use the identification of these deficiencies as starting points from which to identify strategies and behaviors for improving future performances. But use them, don't abuse them. Make note of them—once! Then go on to working on improving: learning new skills, correcting errors, and rehearsing doing things well. Do not dwell on the negative. Replaying poor performances in your head is a way of practicing to perform that poorly again. By giving too much attention to substandard performance, you attribute too much weight to it. This builds expectations of failure, cutting into your confidence. In this way, you may end up acting as if even rare poor performances are the norm and will be a sure thing in the future, thereby making poor performance more likely. In reality, a poor performance need not be indicative of things to come. In fact, one of the nicest things about sports is that you almost always start over with each play, point, shot or event.

Evaluate your performance, not your self. The quality of your performance may be an indication of how well you performed (measured against some criterion), how efficiently you performed, or how fairly you played; but it is not a measure of how good you are, nor need it define your identity. Although your acts are measurable, you, as a total human being, are not. Your value or worth as a person cannot be scientifically or empirically measured. Rather, your value or worth is largely a definitional concept that depends upon your arbitrarily thinking and convincing yourself that you are a "good person" or a "bad person," "worthwhile" or "worthless."

Yet most athletes tend to measure their worth (or at least a large part of it) based on their athletic performances. It is as if they were somehow a good person (or at least a better person) when they perform well and a bad person (or somehow a less important person) when they perform poorly.

It usually is beneficial to observe a poor performance and to acknowledge, for example, that your strategy was poor, your technique inadequate, and your performance subpar. But it is exceptionally foolish and dysfunctional for you to conclude that therefore you are a lousy athlete and an inadequate person who has no worth or capability. Besides being dysfunctional, this is illogical. There is no accurate way of measuring your worth. Attempting to do so inevitably results in overgeneralizations and arbitrary conclusions and definitions. You could not possibly remember all the things you have ever done (even just your performances in athletic competition), assign them relative weights, add them up, and through some mathematical computation come up with some measure of your worth or rating of your self. It would be like adding bananas, apples, and oranges. All you get is fruit salad.

If you rate yourself, sooner or later you tend to feel inadequate, or you may convince yourself falsely that you cannot perform adequately. As a result, you may fail to assert yourself in competition. If you feel you are not worthy of the spoils that go to the victor, of attention, or of winning, or if you feel that it is not OK to win or beat a friend, you may not even do the things it takes to succeed, or you may just go through the motions of doing them. Then your impaired confidence may become a self-fulfilling prophecy.

It is important for you to recognize errors as errors and substandard performances as substandard performances—and nothing more. Mistakes are often inefficient, unproductive, and deleterious to good performance. It is unrealistic, however, for you to overgeneralize and make the groundless conclusion that because you made a mistake or performed poorly that you are a bad person or a worthless athlete.

Your value (to you) as a person accrues to you merely because you are alive. If you accept yourself, you recognize that you invariably have some capability for enjoying yourself, creating happiness and pleasure, and exercising your physical and psychological capacities. You do not have to equate your worth with your achievements (athletic or otherwise) or what others think of you. Nor do you benefit from doing so. Rather, it is preferable not to rate your self at all, but to accept yourself.

Try to get the most out of what you do. Enjoy youself. Enjoy your sport, and master it. Evaluate your athletic (and other) achievements, not your self. It will make it easier to be confident about what you are about to do and feel that you have the right to compete and to do it well.

Act Confidently

Thoughts, feelings, and behaviors all interact, affecting one another. The more you think confidently, the more you feel confident and act confidently. The more you feel confident, the more you think and act confidently. Similarly, the more confidently you act, the more likely you are to think and feel confident.

In the competitive situation, act confidently and look confident. Stand or sit up straight and tall, but relaxed and comfortable, not rigid.

Relaxation is particularly useful in helping you to look and feel confident. Keep your facial muscles loose, keep your movements loose and fluid, and keep nervous activity (fidgeting, preening, wandering, pacing, etc.) to a minimum. Relax. It will help you look and feel calm, collected, and assured.

When you speak, speak clearly, in a normal tone of voice. Avoid getting into conversations about how you feel, the competitors, and the conditions. (These inquiries can be handled with short, polite answers like "Fine," "They are fine athletes," and "The conditions are the same for everyone," accompanied with an easy, relaxed smile.) And do not initiate these kinds of conversations with your opponents. This kind of talk only indicates that you are probably nervous.

Avoid visual eavesdropping of your opponents. Don't stare at them. Let them watch you. Look calm, confident, and ready to go.

Strut your stuff. You need not act brazenly, but you can radiate the message that you know who is going to win.

Even if you have some doubts, act confidently. You will feel more confident if you do. And it may surprise you to find how much others will help you to build on these feelings by the way they respond to a confident-appearing athlete.

Former major league pitcher Gene Conley once described Ted Williams as cutting such an imposing figure and oozing so much confidence that "He took something away from you even before you threw a pitch."[8]

CONCLUSION

Confidence is an important antecedent to good performance. If you are confident, you are more likely to do well. But there is nothing magical about the effects of confidence, nor its acquisition. Behavior is consistent with what we think we are qualified to do, deserve to do, are capable of doing, and are likely to do. As long as expectancies remain high, we are likely to exert a concentrated effort and to persist in the face of adverse circumstances.

Confidence does not just happen to you (or fail to). And it is not something that you have or do not have. Confidence is a state that consists of thinking, acting and feeling confident, all of which can be learned, practiced, intentionally evoked, and made habitual.

Finally, approaching competition confident of victory makes a great deal of sense. It aids performance. Uncertainty and doubt only hinder functioning. And there is no reason to doubt the likelihood of the success of your upcoming performances. In sports, there is no such thing as a sure thing. As Yogi Berra has said, "The game's not over until it's over." Don't doubt what you are not sure about! Approach your performances with confidence!

7

PAIN AND FATIGUE

You learn the pain in practice and will know it in every race. As you approach the limit of your endurance it begins, coming on gradually, hitting your stomach first. Then your arms grow heavy and your legs tighten—thighs first, then knees. You sink, lower in the water because you can't hold yourself up; you are actually swimming deeper in the water, as though someone were pushing down on your back. You experience perception changes. The sounds of the pool blend together and become a crashing roar in your ears. The water takes on a pinkish tinge. Your stomach feels as though it's going to fall out—every kick hurts like hell—and then suddenly you hear a shrill internal scream.

In a race, at the threshhold of pain you have a choice. You can back off—or you can force yourself to drive to the finish. . . . It is right there, at the pain barrier, that the great competitors separate from the rest. Most swimmers back away from the pain! A champion pushes himself on into agony. . . . When it comes it is oddly satisfying because you know it had to come and now it is there, because you are meeting it, taking it without backing down— because you enjoy the triumph of going through it, knowing it is the only way you can win. . . . If you can push yourself through that pain barrier into real agony, you're a champion.[1]

DON SCHOLLANDER

Subjugating oneself to the pain of injury in order to compete has become commonplace in athletics. This is not what this chapter is about. Nor do I recommend using the techniques presented herein for that purpose. The choice whether or not to train or compete in spite of injury is ultimately yours. It should, however, be given careful consideration. And it should be made only after considering the advice of at least one trusted physician who is aware of the demands of your sport.

This chapter is about a different kind of pain. It is about the sensations that result from stressing your muscles and your body's capacity to produce energy. This kind of pain is prevalent in almost all sports. Attempts to build and maintain the strength, speed, and endurance that lay the foundation for superlative performances in most sports necessitate extending your body beyond the limits of physical and psychological comfort. In many sports (swimming, running, and speed skating, for example), levels of performance further hinge on an athlete's ability to push through the pain and fatigue that accompany sustained and/or intense effort. And in almost every sport, at some point, the discomfort of fatigue becomes a factor.

The challenge of managing that pain is made even more formidable by the fact that this pain is self-inflicted. You must push yourself beyond the comfort zone. And it takes continued attention and effort to maintain a level of intensity or speed that hurts. Effort is intentionally produced and sustained. You must continually choose to hurt yourself; otherwise you naturally return to less stressful levels of activity. Keeping the pressure on is no small task.

The painful sensations that accompany physical exertion are variously avoided, retreated from, approached, and sought out. Nobody likes to hurt. Yet nothing makes you feel quite so alive as experiencing the exhilaration that accompanies extending yourself to the limit, feeling the relief and satisfaction that follow optimal exertion, and engaging yourself in meeting the challenge of these internal foes. The physical sensations can be discomforting, if not agonizing. And they can be frightening, even evoking images of dying. But the battle can be intriguing and addicting. Being completely engaged in exercising your capacities to their fullest in order to reach some goal is the ultimate in living and feeling alive. Yet if pushing yourself to the limit is so exhilarating and vitalizing, why do we so often shrink away from exerting ourselves to the optimum and sustaining this effort?

Part of the problem comes from a failure to properly discriminate between sensations that warn of or signal physiological harm and those that accompany optimal utilization of physical attributes or signal growth. Pain can be a signal that something physiologically harmful is happening to you, and thus it usually is sensible to avoid anything even potentially painful and to remove yourself from situations where pain occurs. For example, if you ignored the pain you felt when you put your hand on a hot stove, considerable tissue damage would result. But by avoiding touching hot stoves (or at least by quickly removing your hand when you feel the painful heat) you prevent (or minimize) burning your skin.

Precisely because it is so adaptive (i.e., conducive to survival), you learn early on to avoid pain. You learn to remove yourself from anything painful, to approach painful stimuli tentatively or to avoid them altogether. These strategies protect you from harm.

Because these painful sensations signal harm or hurt, you also learn to label pain as bad. And it is. Signals of physiological harm could hardly be seen as anything but bad.

Unfortunately, the physical sensations that accompany effortful performance are carelessly lumped together with the sensations that warn of or signal physiological harm, both getting labeled pain and being thought of as bad. Furthermore, you generalize your responses to any sensations labeled pain, acting similarly in response to the perception of either. As a result, effortful performances are said to "hurt," and the natural learned response to this pain is to reduce effort, to approach tentatively activities that require effort, or to avoid them altogether.

The pain of optimal exertion is a fairly unique experience. Most nonathletes never hurt in the same way or experience as much physical fatigue at any time in their lives as a serious competitive swimmer, for example, undergoes every day. If you have never experienced these sensations, it is even difficult to comprehend what the experience is like. If you have, it is difficult to adequately portray these feelings to someone else. Though these sensations are difficult to describe, they clearly differ from other kinds of pain. They are readily distinguishable from the pain of injury. They hurt in a different way. Kellen Winslow of the San Diego Chargers has been quoted as saying, "I know what it is to play with pain and to play with injury. There is a big distinction."[2] Anyone who has ever competed with tendinitis, a pulled muscle, knee problems, or even sore muscles would agree that the sensations produced by performing with injuries are very different from those generated by the muscle fatigue and oxygen debt that results from effortful performance. Yet our language fails to help us to differentiate between sensations warning us of danger and those that signal events that are not likely to harm us. Partially because of this linguistic overgeneralization, we respond similarly to these different perceptual phenomena.

Regretfully, avoidance responses to all sensations labeled as pain (though learned and quite natural) are not always functional. This is the case in swimming, running, gymnastics, crew, speed skating, Nordic skiing, and training and competition in many other sports. You do not build strength or endurance nor do you win races by easing up when it starts to hurt, by merely flirting with the pain of effortful response, or by avoiding the pain altogether.

Herein lies the challenge. You learn that pain is "bad." You do not like to hurt. You often fear pain. As a result, you learn to avoid it, often unthinkingly. And when you do experience pain, you tend to automatically retreat from it. But the self-inflicted pain of effortful performance is a necessary component of success. To do well "you gotta hurt." As is often said: "There is no gain without pain."

The challenge is further complicated by the vagaries of our language. We label a wide variety of sensations and experiences as painful. We say it "hurts" when someone criticizes us. It is a "pain" to have to wait in line. It is "painful" to lose. It "hurts" to see a friend unhappy. It is a "pain" when someone or something inconveniences us. It "hurts" to sustain a hard run. And it is "painful" to cut yourself. These "hurts" and "pains" are hardly the same experience. Nevertheless, vastly different phenomena are all labeled as "pain" or "hurt." Anything discomforting, unde-sired, or unpleasant is sometimes seen as painful, and anything called painful is seen as bad, distasteful, and something to be avoided. Consequently, the mere idea that something hurts brings forth associations of many painful events and evokes generalized avoidance responses—avoidance responses that interfere with good athletic performances.

MANAGING PAIN

It is often said that people perceive pain differently due to differ-ent "pain threshholds." It is assumed that some people have low pain threshholds and feel pain from very slight injury, while others have high pain threshholds and feel pain only after intense injury. Experience seems to bear this out—people differ consider-ably in their reported subjective experience of pain and in their tolerance of it. The evidence from laboratory studies, however, indicates that virtually all people experience a sensation at the same level of stimulus input. Clearly, except in rare instances where there is some physical abnormality, differences in pain tolerance are largely psychological, not physiological.

Psychologically, the ability to tolerate pain and perform well in spite of it depends largely on how you appraise the pain, to what you attribute the pain, and how you assess your ability to cope with it. Some strategic employment of images, thought con-trol techniques, relaxation, and imaginal practice will enable you intentionally to handle better your internal challenges and to build good habits for doing so automatically. The key is to inter-pret the painful sensations and to use them in a way that will best help you to perform well and enjoy doing it.

Appraisal

Recalling a number of previous effortful performances, you will note that the experience varies considerably. Sometimes the "pain" of effortful performance feels good. It "hurts," but it is a good kind of hurt. You feel so exhilarated that "pain" gets lost in the joy of the experience. Similarly, sometimes it doesn't seem to hurt much. The pain is qualitatively different. It doesn't seem bad. You notice the painful sensations, but they do not seem to matter. When this is the case, it is easy to put out.

Other times, you struggle. Your awareness of the pain is exaggerated. It seems so much worse, so bad. You fight the pain, and the pain makes it so much more difficult to exert yourself and to maintain any effort you do manage to produce.

Much of the difference in the quality of these experiences stems from how you interpret the physical sensations that accompany your effort. If you label these feelings "pain" and see that pain as something bad, it makes it more difficult to tolerate. If you discount or deemphasize the awfulness of these sensations, their detrimental effects are more easily controlled.

Anything "bad" elicits avoidance reactions and often evokes fear. Pretty soon you find yourself backing off, wondering why you are doing it at all, or having images of getting injured, blacking out, or even of dying.

The moment you label the sensations that accompany effortful performance as something bad, you tend to tighten up. This increased muscular tension further contributes to fatigue and magnifies the intensity with which these sensations are experienced, making it more difficult to continue exerting effort. Usually these reactions are habitual and automatic. The perception of muscle fatigue has been labeled pain, anything painful is seen as bad, and the learned response is to avoid it or back off from it. This sequence is so well ingrained that it requires no thought (though often these kind of thoughts accompany it involuntarily). You just act as if the painful sensations are horrible and begin to catastrophize about their effects.

But you need not view the pain as something bad. You might welcome it instead. There is nothing inherently bad about the sensations. You might just as easily note that the sensations accompanying effortful performance are signs that you are working (that you are building strength, increasing endurance, or challenging the capabilities of your body in a quest for performance excellence) and view these feelings as something positive, perhaps growing pains. Merely reappraising your feelings and relabeling them as "good" will start you on the road to accepting these sensations as a natural part of utilizing your body to its fullest, seeking out these feelings as a signal that you are actively progressing toward your goals, and fading out any tendencies to avoid the "pain."

Learning to view the pain in this new positive manner takes a concerted effort. The old view is well ingrained and hard to change. You need to constantly remind yourself that you need not view the pain as something bad to be feared and avoided (or even begrudgingly borne) or act as if you did. Intentionally welcome these sensations and tell yourself that they are good because they mean you are making progress toward your goals. In this way, you will achieve the "good kind of hurt" more often.

Attribution

To what you attribute the pain is another critical factor determining how you respond to it and ultimately how well you handle it. If you think you are hurting because you are out of shape, "took it out" too fast, did not loosen up enough, or some other thing you did wrong (or is wrong with you), you are pushing the button to back off. Similarly, if you think of the pain as signaling bodily damage, you tend to retreat from it, and it can be scary. It can bring forth images of passing out or even dying in the middle of your effort. The fear tightens you up, exacerbating muscle fatigue and heightening perception of the painful sensations. In turn, the increased tension and the distracting thoughts and images interfere with sustained effort. Pretty soon you find yourself backing off (if you ever managed to close in on a peak effort in the first place).

On the other hand, viewing the pain and fatigue as natural physiological results of effortful performance helps you stay relaxed and leaves the door open for maintaining or increasing your efforts. By accepting these physical sensations as normal, instead of viewing them as horrible or terrible, you more easily read your body, adjust your pace, relax, and utilize your muscles more powerfully, more fluidly, and with greater speed.

Remember that the pain that accompanies effort differs from the pain of injury or illness. It is not a warning of physical harm. It is a natural feeling. Accept the sensations as a normal, expected part of physical exertion. You might do best not even to label these feelings as pain. If you merely see these sensations as signals of a buildup of lactic acid, as oxygen debt, or as muscle fatigue and call them that, it is not quite so bad or so scary.

Assessing Your Ability to Cope

As your muscles go into oxygen debt or approach the limits of their capacity you begin to experience physical sensations that you have learned to label discomforting or painful. Partially because of their similarity to sensations signaling bodily harm, you have learned that they are bad and to be avoided. At the same time, you know they are part of the package that you purchased when investing your efforts toward reaching your goals. You get pulled in two directions: toward increasing or maintaining your efforts in order to reach your goals and toward backing off into the comfort zone. Sometimes you give in and sometimes you push on. Which choice you make depends largely on your expectancy with regard to your ability to withstand the pain and to forge on in spite of it.

Often, when you slow down or ease up it is a result of a vague—or explicit—notion that you cannot take it anymore; or that if you keep it up you will not be able to stand it. You question your ability to tolerate the pain. It is as if you think that the pain will become so terrible, or that your efforts are damaging your body so much, that you may not be able to stand the discomfort or survive the experience. After all, you have heard about runners, cyclists, and swimmers who have dropped dead in the middle of a race. How do you know it won't happen to you? And you are set up for entertaining these notions. Are not any decrements in performance that follow the onset of feelings of fatigue referred to as "dying"?

Admittedly, it is conceivable for someone to extend themselves beyond their physical capacity, putting such a strain on their body that it ceases to function. But especially for a highly conditioned athlete in the absense of physical anomalies or drug ingestion, this seems highly unlikely.

Of course, most often, you do not consciously back off because you really think your effort is going to kill you or that the pain will be so intolerable so as to cause you to black out or die. Often, however, backing off in response to the hurt is a habit that occurs as if you thought that way. More than likely, when you do ease up it is not because you cannot stand the pain you are experiencing at that second. It is not that bad. Rather, your decreased effort probably stems from doubts as to your ability to continue to withstand pain that you think might keep getting worse and become intolerable. Perhaps you are swimming a 1650-yard race and notice after 300 yards that you are "tired." That tiredness is unlikely to raise concern as to your ability to handle the lap you are on or even that 100, but it easily evokes thoughts questioning your ability to cope with the painful sensations of continued fatigue or questioning the utility of continuing to exert yourself when, judging from the early signs of fatigue, you expect you will fail to do well anyway. Similarly, the assessment of fatigue may elicit images of dying (figuratively or perhaps even literally) later on in the race. So in response to catastrophic thoughts, to images of not finishing, falling over dead, or experiencing unbearable agony, or out of habit that these thoughts and images have already created, you bail out before you reach the real limit. Former football great Jim Brown says, "The fear of fatigue is the greatest fear of all. If you fear you will run out of stamina, you can never be truly effective."[3] Now that is not to say that muscle fatigue doesn't take its toll, hampering your ability to keep the pressure on. Obviously, it does. But you rarely get to the point where performance diminishes purely as a result of the physiological effects of fatigue. Much more often, you lose it psychologically before you do physically. But you need not back off in anticipation of not being able to handle future pain. Stay in the present. Deal with what is occurring immediately. Take it one lap, one instant, one play at a time.

Nor does pain or fatigue need to serve as a signal to slow down or decrease effort (either intentionally or automatically). I had a memorable and educative experience in a dual meet in college. I had just swum a grueling 1000-yard freestyle, where I had "sucked it up" and gone after the leader with 200 yards remaining, sprinting the rest of the way. The premeet strategy was for me to come back and swim the 500-yard freestyle, but as the meet progresses the coach came to think that our only chance of winning the meet was if I could swim and win the 200-yard butterfly as well as the 500. In those days, many swimmers viewed a 200 fly with great trepidation. It was expected to hurt. My experience with swimming a 200 fly was that I would usually get out pretty well. I would be swimming fairly loose and strong when I would notice how good I felt and wonder when my arms were going to start to hurt. Sure enough, at that moment my attention would zero in on my arms and they would start to hurt. Then, I would inevitably sink in the water, slow down, and struggle the rest of the way. On this particular day, I was still feeling the effects of the 1000. I remember, while on the starting block, explicitly telling myself, "Now I don't need to worry about when my arms are going to start to hurt—they *already* hurt." Feeling relieved, I was able to focus on what I was doing and had a good swim.

While experience made a distinct impression on me and helped me to better swims, it was not until many years later that I was able to benefit fully from the experience. Right away, I was able to see the futility of worrying about the pain and to realize that the pain was not that bad and that I could take it. But only later did I realize that in these and many similar instances, I was slowing down out of a habit that was based on the assumption that if I hurt (or got tired) I had to slow down. By challenging the assumption that I could not swim fast even if I hurt with counters such as "So what if it hurts, that's no reason to slow down" coupled with instructions to "Stay with it" or "Pick it up," the pain has ceased to be a signal to slow down.

Pain need not act as a cue signaling a decrease in effort. Easing up on the pressure is a habit, not a necessary reaction. It is a habit easily acquired in our culture, but you can learn instead to use the pain as a signal to stay with it and increase your effort. You even can learn to keep the pressure on when experiencing the "bad kind of hurt." With practice, habits can be forged. Eventually, you can get to the point where anytime you begin to hurt, you will automatically increase your effort or pick up the pace. Bjorn Borg has arrived at a point where he says, "It does not matter if I am so tired that I do not think I can take one more step, I will not give up that point . . . I will keep going."[4]

Of course, at any given time your ability to maintain or increase your speed or intensity of response will be determined by the work you previously have put in (or failed to put in). While both your immediate performance and preparation through training are affected by your skill in handling the discomfort, good psychology will not substitute for physical training. You must do the work.

Relaxation

Relaxation is a major step in managing the pain. The more relaxed you are in the muscles you are not using, the less energy you burn up and the more you delay fatigue. Relaxation also leads to experiencing the pain less intensely and to finding these sensations less disturbing.

Relaxation further helps to keep you calm. Expectations concerning pain increase anxiety, which in turn fosters muscle tension, leading to more pain and consequently more anxiety. This cycle can be interrupted by relaxation. If you are relaxed, you are less likely to worry about hurting and less likely to panic at the perception of fatigue.

When you do experience the painful sensations that accompany effortful performance, use them as a cue to relax as well as to pick up your pace or intensify your effort. Increased effort necessarily involves increased muscular tension. Thus you must differentially relax unneeded muscle groups while tensing the appropriate muscles.

Attention Diversion

One method commonly employed in an attempt to manage pain is to divert your attention from the pain. Some runners report focusing on objects in the physical environment to the exclusion of the noxious sensations. Others report doing complicated math problems or imaginally building houses from scratch in order to get through "the wall" during a marathon.

Some athletes "go somewhere else in their head" psychologically removing themselves from the pain. For example, one might imaginally relive an experience incompatible with experiencing pain, perhaps peacefully lying on a tropical beach on a warm summer day. (This means of getting away from the discomfort was graphically demonstrated in the television movie *Tribes*).

These diversionary tactics may have some degree of effectiveness, but they have their limitations. Optimal effort is not easily sustained. It requires almost continual monitoring of bodily functions and frequent initiation of increased effort. If your head is somewhere else, you are likely to be less attentive to these demands and performance level can readily fall off. Particularly in the endurance events it is important to pay attention to the signals your body gives you. This information is useful for pacing yourself, conserving energy through efficient performance, preventing injury, and maximizing speed. A marathon runner may be able to cruise on automatic, but the best runners report paying close attention to their bodies rather than drifting off.

Attention diversion is additionally problematic where you need to be attentive to cues from the environment. Even in swimming where most of the cues that guide performance are internal, you still need to be aware enough of your surroundings to judge your turns.

Still, imagination can be employed to enhance your motivation to push yourself to the limits and to enhance your ability to successfully manage the physical byproducts of that effort. But it works best when strategically combined with a careful reading of your body. Many of you will find it easier to get after it by imaginally transforming a practice run into the Boston Marathon, a swimming repeat into an Olympic final, or a lonely skate into a World Championship race.

Use your imagination to make your efforts more challenging, more exhilarating and more enjoyable, not to escape the experience you came to have. Attention diversion techniques presume that you cannot take the pain and need to hide from it. These sensations are a natural part of extending yourself to the limits. Welcome them. Experience the whole adventure. It is an exciting challenge.

Countering

When you start to feel the byproducts of your effort you may have thoughts or images that are distracting, evoke fear, increase tension, impair motivation, or otherwise decrease the likelihood of your staying with it. You may respond to the perception of the painful sensations with thoughts such as "I'm tired," "My arms hurt," "I can't take it," "I'm sucking air already," "Why am I doing this?" "Can I make it?" or images of "cratering," falling apart, experiencing unbearable pain, passing out, or having a heart attack.

Challenge these ideas and images with thoughts and images more facilitative of reaching your goals. Take care to notice that the deleterious messages are often hidden behind the words or mental pictures. "I'm tired" may be an accurate assessment of how you feel, but what needs to be countered is the message it brings with it: that your feeling tired is a cause for decreased levels of performance. Attack that idea with thoughts like "So what? That doesn't mean I need to slow down. Pick it up!" Similarly, "My arms hurt" implies that their hurting is bad and, again, is a cause for backing off the pressure. Challenge these ideas with thoughts like "Good! I must be building strength. Keep it up!"

"Why am I doing this?" is a rhetorical question disguising the statement that you shouldn't subject yourself to this awful pain. Tell yourself, "It's not that bad," that "you really do want to do it" (if necessary, cite your goals and their personal importance), and to "get after it."

"Can I make it?" is another rhetorical question disguising a catastrophic message. It means something like "The pain will probably become so unbearable that I won't be able to take it." Like the message "I can't take it," this idea can be countered with "Who says I can't?" or "Where is the evidence I can't?" coupled with instructions to "stay with it and do the best you can" or to "take it one moment at a time. It never gets that bad. It is the anticipation that is hard to take."

"I'm sucking air already" also may be an accurate observation, but it sneakily implies that something must be wrong with you and that you will necessarily fail to keep providing your body with the needed fuel. That is possible. But it may be that you are breathing hard unnecessarily and may be able to relax, calm down, and get into the rhythm. Try it. You have little to lose.

Images of experiencing unbearable pain, passing out, having a heart attack or other physical catastrophies that evoke fear should be replaced with images of successfully coping with the fatigue, thoughts questioning the likelihood of such "horrors," and reminders of your good state of health and high level of conditioning. (This, of course, necessitates adequate physical preparation for strenuous competitive undertakings!)

Images of "cratering" or falling apart serve as predictions of what is likely (often even acting as self-fulfilling prophecies). Replace them with images of getting home strong, relaxing and building your effort, or revitalized energetic performances. These images will better ward off panic, foster confidence, and direct your efforts.

Turn around your dysfunctional reactions to pain. They need not impede performance if you head them off at the pass.

A WORD OF CAUTION

The techniques presented in this chapter for managing pain are recommended for use by highly conditioned athletes in their struggle to stretch the limits of their bodies during their quest for superlative performance. Many of these techniques may also be applied by those of you who are attempting to better condition your bodies. Some caution, however, should be advised. Pain is your body's way of telling you when something is wrong. You must learn to read your body well enough to discriminate between those times when you must heed the warnings of pain in order to prevent physiological damage and those times when you may push on. As Bill Koch, Olympic cross-country skier, says, "You go as fast as your body can tolerate. . . . But you learn your limits and know them well."[5]

CONCLUSION

Pain and fatigue are among the most overwhelming obstacles to superlative preparation and performance in many sports. Tolerating pain and preventing it from interfering with performance is a formidable psychological challenge. Fatigue is a real physical detriment to performance, but most often it is preceded and exacerbated by its psychological impact.

Much of the problem lies in the tendency to view the pain and fatigue of effortful performance as something bad and as a signal to back off from the pressure. Meeting the challenge begins with challenging these assumptions and forming new habits.

Old habits are hard to change. These transformations are especially difficult. When your body is knotting up and screaming for oxygen, it is difficult to think clearly and to remember to interpret the experience in new ways and employ new strategies. As a result, I recommend imaginally practicing coping with these sensations in a quiet time when you are removed from the actual physiological effects of effortful performance, in addition to intentionally employing these new strategies as opportunities arise.

Whether imaginally or during actual performance, when it starts to hurt, relax. Remind yourself that the pain is not so bad and that you can take it. Stay in the present, handling it as it comes. It never gets as bad as you might fear it will.

Stop viewing pain and fatigue as something bad to be feared, avoided, or retreated from. Instead, view these sensations as your allies—signs that you are working hard, building strength, gaining stamina, and going fast or strong.

Use these sensations as signals to relax, stay loose, stretch it out, stay with it, and pick it up. There is no reason why they need to be signals to back off or slow down.

Perhaps the best strategy of all is to divorce these sensations from all your other associations to things called pain or hurt. Relabel these sensations as partial muscle fatigue, oxygen debt, or the buildup of lactic acid. These labels do not sound so scary and have few negative associations. In fact, they do not have to be scary or bad at all. As Lothar Kipke, the East German national team physician for 20 years and head of the Institute for Sports Medicine in Leipzig, recently told me: "There is no pain in sport. Pain is when they [the athletes] are sick or injured. Pain is bad. Sports are fun. They never go together."[6]

8

ANXIETY

I didn't feel much pressure the night before the game, when the manager told me that even if Guidry went only a third of an inning I'd be the next guy out there. But I felt the pressure when I actually came into the game. More pressure than I've ever felt. . . . I tried to calm myself down by thinking of the mountains of Colorado, the mountains I love. I thought that the worst thing that could happen to me was that I'd be in those mountains tomorrow.[1]

GOOSE GOSSAGE

Anxiety is one of the most common deterrents to good performance. At worst, the effects of anxiety get you so tied up in knots that you are frozen in fear. At best, anxiety subtly impairs performance by distracting your attention.

That is not to say that you cannot produce superlative performances when nervous. You can. In fact, most athletes experience some anxiety before producing their top performances. However, these superlative efforts come in spite of the anxiety, not because of it. By its nature, anxiety tends to interfere with athletic performance.

THE NATURE OF ANXIETY

When you get anxious your heart rate increases, your blood pressure becomes elevated, your breathing becomes more rapid, and oxygen consumption increases. You may experience nausea, light-headedness, dryness of the mouth, or feelings of fatigue or weakness. You may yawn frequently, begin to tremble, or engage in nervous activity (bite your nails, wiggle your leg, twirl your hair, etc.). You may sweat profusely, urinate frequently, or have loose stools. You may have difficulty getting to sleep. And you inevitably have an increase in muscular tension. You may even have difficulty in breathing as the muscles of your neck and throat tense up causing you to choke (literally and figuratively).

THE EFFECTS OF ANXIETY

Weak or wobbly legs, an increased heart rate, and increased oxygen consumption obviously can accelerate fatigue. Perhaps the most deleterious physical symptom of anxiety, however, is increased muscular tension. Tension in antagonistic muscles interferes with the smooth functioning of needed muscle groups. It impairs the speed and force with which you can use your muscles. Excessive tension contributes to early fatigue. It heightens awareness of the self-inflicted pain accompanying effortful performance.

These effects of anxiety are typified by what Frank Satterwaite has to say about fellow squash player Stu Goldstein: "Stu is cat-quick and incredibly fit, and he's totally dedicated to improving himself as a player. But he's a little brittle—both physically and psychologically. Perhaps because he's *so intense*, he gets more than his share of muscle pulls, and he sometimes gets so tight in a match, his game snaps."[2]

Anxiety takes it toll psychologically as well as physically. It results in a narrowing of the perceptual field and of your attentional focus. You become less capable of taking in and processing information. And you tend to lack flexibility. As a result, you have greater difficulty adjusting to unanticipated events and you tend to become confused more easily.

Instead of focusing on the task at hand, when anxious you tend to become overburdened with yourself. You tend to focus on and worry about the physical symptoms of anxiety. You may become acutely aware of your heart pounding. Or you may zero in on your "nervous stomach." In fact, often it is not the arousal per se, but rather the attention to and worry about the arousal that is debilitating to performance.

When anxious, you also tend to observe and evaluate how well you are doing and how good you are. This kind of self-referential worry interferes with good play. When busy judging yourself against your expectations and comparing yourself with others, you cannot attend to the game.

Furthermore, when you are anxious you may be overwhelmed with the intrusion of distracting and maladaptive thoughts and images. You tend to focus on all the things that may go wrong, how inadequate or incapable you are, how poorly you might do, and the consequences of possible substandard performances. These thoughts and images are good practice for performing poorly. And they are distracting. As a result, they tend to become self-fulfilling prophecies. You become more likely to perform just as poorly as you feared you might.

One of the most disrupting influences of anxiety is its tendency to elicit thoughts of avoidance and escape. When you perceive some danger and lack confidence in your ability to cope with it, you naturally look for ways to hide or escape from it and reasons to do so. Thoughts like "I don't really want it" or "Who cares?" as well as cognitive searches for ways out ("Coach, I don't feel well") and preprepared excuses (just in case you fail) may seemingly protect you from some perceived danger associated with performance, but they assuredly impair motivation and enjoyment.

SOURCES OF ANXIETY

Nowhere is an individual's performance more closely scrutinized by so many people than in the world of sports. The results of an athlete's efforts are immediately available to be judged against the clearest of criteria by sometimes as many as thousands of people, with millions more watching on television and listening to the radio.

As if that were not enough pressure, an athlete's performance may be replayed, described, analyzed, questioned, and critiqued by the media, and may even be the source of political propaganda. Furthermore, athletes invest years of labor and countless dollars in preparation. And the outcome of a contest, individual performances, and collective statistics often make the difference in job security, prestige, and recognition, thousands and sometimes millions of dollars in prize money and salaries, opportunities for lucrative endorsement contracts, and countless other rewards and privileges.

The thrill of the competition is still there. But the pressure to perform can be immense and profered from multitudinous sources. And yet if anxiety is to be a factor, you need to buy what is being sold. It does not necessarily come with the territory. For it is not the close scrutiny, the opportunity for massive gains, the huge investment on the line, the impending critique, or the encouragements (or threats) from others that make you nervous. It is your perception and interpretation of these events that lead to anxiety.

Anxiety comes from a way of looking at the world in general or events in particular and a way of thinking about these things.

Most often it comes from unrealistic, exaggerated, and always futile ways of thinking. It is not the contest that gets you nervous, but the way you view it.

Worry

Worry lies at the root of anxiety. The more you worry, the more the nervous tension grows. It is all too easy to fall into the trap of believing that worrying will somehow ward off danger or at least insure adequate preparation. Unfortunately, it does not work that way. Worrying about how well prepared you are or how well you stack up against others does not help you get any better prepared, it only engenders anxiety.

That is not to say that it is not useful to plan and cognitively rehearse for future events. Of course it is. That is precisely what the bulk of this book is about. But there is a difference between planning and rehearsal on the one hand and worry on the other. Worry consists of ruminating about undesirable events and outcomes. It in no way enhances your ability to control them. It is a passive activity. Planning and rehearsal actively and effectively impact your control.

When we worry, we tend to focus on the undesirable aspects of our activities and the negative consequences that might result. And we tend to blow things out of proportion. We act as if things might be so terrible or awful that we would not be able to stand them.

Most of the time, we do not get explicit with ourselves about what would be so terrible, but we act as if some vague, unspecified terrible result might accrue. It is that catastrophizing that engenders anxiety.

Much of our worrying comes in the "What if . . . ?" variety. We raise issues like "What if I lose?" "What if I don't make the team?" "What if I can't finish?" "What if I blow it?" or "What if I don't do my best time?" without bothering to actually answer these "What ifs." Instead, the "What ifs" implicitly tell us that some unspecified, terrible danger is looming.

Sometimes even the "What if" is hidden, making it still harder to recognize how we are getting ourselves nervous. Statements like "This is the big one!" "This is it!" "This is my last chance!" sidestep the "What if" and directly imply "I have to make it, and if I don't, it will be terrible."

Those times that we do identify what might happen, we also tend to exaggerate the odds of the worst occurring. Sometimes we get worried about even the most unlikely of undesirable events—

events whose odds of occurrence would stagger the imagination of a statistician. Zeroing in thoughts on some unlikely, undesirable event and thinking about it as if it were a sure thing only arouses anxiety.

Just thinking about negative consequences gives them an air of reality and psychologically increases the odds of their occurrence. The more you dwell on them, the more real they become.

Even worrying about worrying or about the physical symptoms of anxiety becomes the source of additional anxiety. Here again, it is the catastrophic nature of worrying that is the source of anxiety. You notice you are nervous, and then worry about your nervousness—as if it were terrible to worry or feel nervous, or as if your nervousness insured poor performances (which, of course, you think will lead to some terrible consequences)—only to get even more nervous, thereby exacerbating the problem. This kind of doomsaying can act like a snowball rolling down a hill quickly turning into an avalanche.

The ironic thing is that in most cases you have made a mountain out of a molehill. There are very few real negative consequences accruing from poor performances in the world of sports. In most instances, a poor performance merely results in a missed opportunity to get some of the rewards that come from doing well. That, of course, is disappointing. But it hardly warrants the fear and avoidance behaviors that come with catastrophizing about poor performances resulting in aversive consequences. You might merely miss a chance to get something good. You rarely face the prospect of having something terrible happen to you. Nor is the activity usually terrible (even the "pain" of effortful performance is not that bad). Nevertheless, a major source of anxiety is this mistaken view of possible missed opportunities to get something good as chances to get something bad.

Of course, sometimes it seems like something terrible might happen. And in fact, most athletes do punish themselves for poor performances with a loss of self-esteem. Which brings me to the major source of precompetitive anxiety: the equation of self-worth with performance.

Rating Your Self

Especially in the United States, we tend to equate what we do with who or what we are. It is as though if we perform well, we are somehow a better or more superior person, and if we do poorly, we are somehow less worthy or more inadequate. Other people act that way toward us. When we perform well on the athletic field we are treated as if we were somehow special or superior individuals. When we flop, people act as though there is something lacking in the very essence of our being. And we treat ourselves that way. We let our feelings toward ourselves bounce up and down with the quality of our performances like yoyos. When performances fall short of the standards we set for ourselves, we tend to get down on ourselves, as if there were something wrong with us for not performing well. When we play poorly we tend to feel inadequate and inferior. We criticize and condemn ourselves. And we anticipate a loss of status and esteem in society.

No wonder people get nervous before a sporting event. If your worth, your value to yourself, or your image of yourself depends on how well you do, the performance situation can be extremely scary. Instead of vying for a good performance, a medal, prize money, or championship honors, you are contesting your worth. If you do well, you are OK. If not, you are not.* The threat to how you feel about yourself posed by your worth being on the line in the competition can be vast. As a result, instead of enthusiastically anticipating the chance to perform, you end up nervously approaching (or avoiding) it because your fear failure.

MANAGING ANXIETY

Most often anxiety stems from inappropriate and futile ways of looking at the situation. As such, a major part of managing anxiety lies in changing your way of thinking. Sometimes, however, an athlete may experience anxiety because he has not trained well, or at all, for an event. It would be foolish, in these instances, to focus on the anxiety. The anxiety would probably be more easily remedied by better preparation and harder training. Certainly performance would be better served this way.

A good test of whether anxiety is interfering with your competitive performance is to compare how well you do in various situations. Usually, if you are performing more poorly in competition than in practice, or more poorly in major competitions than in less important competitions, it is a good indication that anxiety may be the culprit. Then more diligent preparation may not suffice (though it always helps). You may need to turn to other methods of managing anxiety.

---

*Even the fan seems to think he is somehow better if his team wins.

Strive for Perfection,
Don't Demand It

Begin by making sure you have set realistic goals. You may be getting yourself anxious by pressuring yourself to compete at a level that you do not have the ability to handle or master at the time. It may be a little painful or disappointing to have to realistically reassess your abilities. But resetting your standards may relieve some pressure, freeing you up to perform at higher levels.

This can be a subtle venture. You do not want to limit yourself. You want to reach for the stars and strive for perfect performances. Yet you do not ever want to demand perfection. Give yourself confidence by predicting perfection. Direct your behavior by being satisfied with nothing less than perfection. But be pleased with improvements. Demanding perfection creates too much pressure. It implies that if you fall short of perfect, which you inevitably will, there is something wrong with you. A demand says you should do it, even though you know you cannot always come through. The irrational demand to do the impossible only adds up to pressure.

Strive for perfection, but remind yourself that even the most superlative performances are not perfect. That takes some of the pressures off. I consider Bob Beamon's long jump in the 1968 Mexico City Olympics to be one of the most extraordinary athletic feats (if not *the* most extraordinary) in history. Yet even that was not a perfect jump. If nothing else, he did not hit the takeoff board perfectly. There is always room for improvement. Sooner, or later, someone will jump even farther. Even now, at this writing, Carl Lewis is mounting a challenge to Beamon's world record.

Nadia Comaneche has led the way to a recent wave of perfect 10 scores in gymnastics competitions. Greg Louganis similarly received many tens in his diving career. Yet even these so-called perfect scores do not reflect perfect performances. To a very large extent they are relative marks. Slow-motion analyses would reveal slight imperfections in even these great performances. As diving coach Hobie Billingsley says, "There is no perfect dive."[3]

In most sports the difference between even the greatest of performances and perfection is vast. No one ever bats 1.000 for the season. Nor does anyone expect to. Yet most baseball players tend to expect (demand—not predict!) to get a hit each individual time they go to bat, and certainly every time in the clutch. They forget that collective statistics come from many individual performances. Thus, they act as if there is something wrong with them, someone else, or the world in general when they fail to come through. Why else would Reggie Jackson throw his bat into the dugout after being struck out by Bob Welch in a critical moment in the 1977 World Series? Of course, he was disappointed. But the anger only comes as a result of demanding that he get a hit. So, too, does the nervousness that hinders getting the very hit that is so important. In this case, Reggie's nervousness contributed to his getting distracted by Bucky Dent's breaking for second base on the pitch.

A lot of the pressure can be taken off by reminding yourself that in many situations and in the long run you need not perform perfectly to win. A baseball player would have to fail to get a hit 6 out of every 10 at bats in order to hit .400. A major leaguer would have to fail to hit a home run 438 times out of 500 at bats, or approximately 7 out of every 8 chances, in order to hit 62 dingers in a season. Yet either of those statistics would be a sure ticket to the Hall of Fame.

When I work with golfers I have them imagine that they hit a good drive, a good approach shot, a good chip, and a good putt on every shot in an imaginary round. I tell them to imagine their good shots, not even their unusually good ones, let alone ones they have yet to hit. Then I ask them what they would shoot for 18 holes, if all of their shots were good. Most of the professional or collegiate golfers I work with usually come up with a figure somewhere around 54. Now, no one shoots a 54! And you do not have to. If you consistently shot in the high 60s, you would be a leading money winner on the pro tour. That leaves a lot of room for imperfection. Remaining cognizant of that helps keep you loose.

Accept Some Nervousness as Natural

You will probably never totally eliminate anxiety in the performance situation. Nor do you need to in order to perform well. How anxiety affects your performance depends on what you do with it.

A certain amount of nervousness is likely, but accept it and use it. Keep it from getting out of hand and interfering with your performance. Don't make it worse by worrying and catastrophizing about it.

When you feel yourself getting anxious, use those feelings as an ally: a cue to cope. Tell yourself to stay calm. And remind yourself that some mild tension need not be detrimental. If you have put in the training, your skills will be well practiced enough to plug in automatically and you will be strong enough and in good enough shape to overcome any hindering effects that mild tension might have on strength, speed and endurance. Remind yourself of this.

It often helps to relabel this arousal as excitement or anticipation rather than anxiety or nervousness. This simple relabeling tends to get you eagerly looking forward to the challenge rather than wanting to get it over with or hoping you will get rained out. And such relabeling tends to prevent any escalation of symptoms.

Use these feelings as signals to take positive action. They can be a reminder that how well you do is important to you and warrants precise, focused attention.

More importantly, use the feelings of anxiety as a signal to relax. If you relax, you cannot get anxious about feeling nervous.

Relax

You cannot be tense, nervous, and relaxed at the same time. Relaxation, by its very nature, keeps your muscles loose, your heart rate down, and oxygen consumption to a minimum. It helps keep you calm and rational and tends to keep you from catastrophizing.

Intentionally plug in deep-muscle relaxation. And employ your differential relaxation skills. It is important that you minimize the tension in muscles that are antagonistic to the muscles you will need. This will help you delay fatigue and increase power, speed, grace, and flexibility.

If there is time before an event, take an imaginal trip to some peaceful, pleasant setting. This will keep your head busy, preventing you from worrying. And it will help you stay relaxed.

You might find it helps to keep your mind off worrisome thoughts by engaging in other relaxing activities. When waiting for an event, you might get absorbed in some music you like. The psychologist for the Soviet National swimming team prepares a book of jokes and humorous anecdotes for individual swimmers to read while they are waiting to swim in major competitions. You might similarly read something light. Vasili Alexeyev, Olympic champion weightlifter, says he loves to play dominoes before a competition "because it destroys the cares that come then."[4] I have even resorted to telling the timers jokes at the starting block as a way of relieving tension before a big race. Whatever works to keep you loose, relaxed, and unconcerned (unconcerned—not uncaring!) about the consequences of your performance, do it.

At the very least, you can always instruct yourself to "relax" and employ some breathing techniques. Former basketball star Bob Petit said that he relaxed "before shooting a free throw by taking a deep breath, then slowly letting the air out of his lungs."[5]

Self-Instructional Methods

Self-instructional methods are an effective way to invoke a relaxation response. Merely telling yourself, "Stay calm!" "Relax!" "Be cool!" "Poise!" "Act confident!" or the like can have a tremendous calming effect.

You may choose to take a few minutes to assess the task that lies before you by asking yourself some questions about what it is you want to do and then answering these questions. This kind of action-oriented, goal-directed thinking can be a nice substitute for the self-referential worrying that might otherwise occur. Gymnast Kurt Thomas controlled his anxiety by thinking "about my routines and not about what the other guy scored or what I was scoring, but mainly about what I have to do when I get up there."[6] Diver Jenny Chandler employed a similar strategy in her 1976 Olympic springboard championship performance. "I didn't look at the scoreboard," Chandler revealed. "If I watch the scores it makes me too nervous. . . . I try not to think about anything but the dive I'm doing."[7]

Thoughts that elicit plans for directing your actions to best handle the idosyncracies of the immediate situation may be of particular utility. But avoid catastrophizing about imperfect conditions. Emphasize positive coping actions. Worrying about the fans, the lights, the weather, and so on only gets you tight. Planning to best handle conditions gets you prepared.

Limit your immediate pregame planning and imaginal practice to a few things you need to focus on for this particular event or under these unique conditions. But do not spend a lot of time engaged in this kind of thinking just prior to competing. This is not the time for instructional preparation and practice. You should get that done ahead of time. This is the time to relax and enjoy yourself. Too much attention devoted to the upcoming event is likely to invite some worrying about the outcome.

What Is the Worst
That Can Happen?

Anxiety largely consists of worry about yourself and various outcomes of events. Whether explicit, implied, or just a vague feeling, anxiety reflects the fear or expectation that something terrible is going to happen that you cannot control and will not be able to cope with. These expectations are usually unrealistic. And it is never useful to look at things this way. It only gets you anxious, which feels crumby and impairs your ability to perform at your best.

Counter these beliefs that are at the root of anxiety. Start by getting specific about the "terrible" thing you fear. Ask yourself, "What is the worst that can happen?" If you do poorly, are you going to die? Are you going to be in excruciating pain? Is someone going to say they are disappointed in you? Are you going to fail to make the team? Are you going to fail to finish? Will you make a mistake, thereby demonstrating to all the world that you are imperfect? Exactly what is it that is so scary? What is the worst thing that can possibly happen?

Usually, it is the perceived awfulness of a vague and unspecified possible outcome that produces the fear. It is difficult to cope with the unknown. When you get specific, even the most undesirable events realistically do not look that bad. If nothing else, when you specify your fears you can also devise strategies for coping.

How Bad Is It, Really?

Once you have gotten a handle on what possible consequence is getting you anxious, ask yourself how bad it really would be. Despite pronouncements like "Defeat is worse than death—you don't have to live with death," "Losing is like dying," and "losing isn't like dying—it's worse," the consequences of poor performances are not really that terrible.

So what if someone else is disappointed in you? You would rather not have that happen. But is it terrible? Does it make you bad?

So what if you make a mistake? You strive for perfection. It is exciting and rewarding to perform almost flawlessly. But mistakes are not catastrophes. They would only prove you are not perfect. But who *is* perfect? Imperfection does not make you inadequate or inferior, merely human!

Take a look at your worst fears and ask yourself how bad they would be. Ask yourself what it is you realistically have to lose. Ask yourself what bad things you might get or what ills might befall you. In most cases in sports, when you perform more poorly than you would have liked to or fail to reach your goals, you merely miss an opportunity to get something good. You rarely suffer adverse consequences.

Naturally, it is always disappointing to miss an opportunity to experience the thrill of playing "out of your head" or to reap the rewards and satisfactions of doing well. But not getting something good is not the same as getting something bad.

Keep each contest in its proper perspective. Don't let the threat of possible disappointment quell your excitement or prevent you from eagerly anticipating the chance to compete.

If you do poorly, it is not the end of the world. Especially if you have made a point of enjoying your training and other competitions, this one event need not be that precious. You really have nothing to lose (except the opportunity). And you have much to gain.

Rod Laver says he frequently employed this strategy: "The thing that always worked best for me whenever I felt I was getting too tense to play good tennis was to simply remind myself that the worst thing—the very worst thing—that could happen to me was that I'd lose a bloody tennis match. That's all."[8]

How Likely Is the Worst?

Dwelling on your fears makes them seem more real and more likely to come true. Before your worries lead you to act as if the worst is inevitable, examine your fears and ask yourself how likely they really are.

Will your parents really kill you if you don't do your best time? What are the odds of the coach kicking you off the team if you miss this free throw? Will you lose all chances at a scholarship and necessarily have to do menial labor for the rest of your life if you play poorly today while the college coach is in the stands? Some of these things might happen, but how likely are they? Most of the things you fear are highly improbable, don't treat them as if they were sure to occur.

Counter Anxiety: Engendering Thoughts

Once you have taken a good, hard, realistic look at what the worst things are that can happen, how bad they really are, and how likely they are to actually occur, you are in a good position to effectively counter anxiety-engendering thoughts as they occur. Feeling nervous should act as a cue that you are viewing the situation in an unrealistic and maladaptive way. Use these feelings as a signal to plug in relaxation, take more useful perspectives, and counter negative thinking.

Most counters will be directed at putting the competitive situation back in its proper perspective by discounting the awfulness of not doing well. Thus, a "What if . . . ?" or "I'm nervous" can be effectively countered with a simple "So what? It's not terrible and it's not likely. So, why worry? Worrying is not useful."

Hidden under even such diverse thoughts like "I should have worked harder," "I'll never win this," "I gotta win," or "They look so big" is the message "Something terrible is going to happen that I won't be able to cope with." These thoughts can be countered with statements reassuring yourself that you can do well, that you can manage any anxiety without getting nervous about it and making it worse, and that it would not be terrible if you did fail.

Thus, "I should have worked harder—I'll never win this" can be countered with "Yes, it probably would have helped if I worked harder. But that doesn't mean I can't win now. And if I don't, it's not terrible, I'll just have to work harder in preparation for next time. In any case, it is not useful to focus on my shortcomings. It only gets me anxious and impairs my confidence. Think about the things you did do that will help you do well."

"I gotta win" can be handled with a "No! I don't have to win. But I'd like very much to win. So give it all you've got."

"They look so big" is a way of saying "We can't beat them—and it's going to be awful when we lose." You might challenge those ideas with a simple "So what?" implying that just because they are so big doesn't mean they'll win. And even if they did, it would not be terrible."

It always helps to remind yourself that this kind of thinking is not useful. It only gets you anxious and distracts you from the task. But do not worry about negative thinking. It is normal and will occur. Nevertheless, you do not have to pay attention to it. Let it go in one ear and out the other. Or use it as a cue to think more positively. Everyone, even the most successful athletes, has doubts and other maladaptive thoughts. For the most part, however, they do not make a big deal of them. They merely redirect their thoughts more functionally and proceed to take care of business.

Contest Your Sport, Not Your Self

Underlying almost all of the awfulness in the prospect of doing poorly is the equation of self-worth with performance. The perceived menace rarely comes from possible impending unpleasant consequences, but from knowing that you will feel like a failure if you fail.

Remind yourself that you are not what you do. How well you perform in no way reflects how good, bad, valuable, invaluable, worthy, worthless, adequate, inadequate, superior, or inferior you are. If you do well, that's good. It often literally feels good. It is satisfying, and there are lots of rewards. If you miss, you miss. That is too bad. But it is not terrible. And certainly, neither are you.

If you approach your sport as if your performance will be a measure of your self, you get nervous. You start to look for a way out of having to put yourself on the line. You become afraid of failure. You strive to avoid losing instead of striving to win. And you tend to constantly monitor how well you are doing instead of paying attention to what you are doing.

When you do fail, you look for excuses. Excuses become a way of protecting your self-image. Subsequently, you may even start to look for excuses in advance. Then you seemingly cannot fail. You have provided yourself with the mirage of built-in protection.

But there is no shame in failure. Failures can be important learning experiences. And they only demonstrate your imperfection. As Mark Lieberman, one of America's most successful wrestlers, recently said, "I think it's important that people know you fail. It shows you're human. When you hide your losses, it makes you afraid to lose."[9]

There may be some benefits in others thinking you are invincible. And you need not approach your sport thinking it is OK to lose. It is not OK. The object of any sport is to win. That challenge is what makes sports so exciting. But you must know you are OK even if you fail. There is a big difference!

Relish the Chance to Compete

Too much worrying not only gets you anxious, but leads you to forget why you are competing in the first place: Sports are fun!

Approach each contest as an opportunity to exercise the skills and conditioning you have worked so hard to develop. At any given moment you are as prepared as you are. Whatever level that is, here is your chance to use it. Here is an opportunity to engage yourself completely in the quest of some goal.

Winning or losing is important, but the thrill, the excitement, the ultimate high are in the playing. Nothing makes you feel quite so alive as exercising every fiber of your existence as you push for the ultimate performance. The measures of that performance determine the winner and perhaps your level of satisfaction. But the experience itself is what sports are all about. That excitement transcends the products of the experience.

If you will approach your sport with that goal in mind (to put all you can into it and to enjoy it), you cannot get anxious. Rather you will relish every opportunity to compete. The process, not the results, will be the primary attraction. And paradoxically, your nonconcern for the results will help you perform even better.

CONCLUSION

I remember how I used to take the train to Stockholm every day after school to play, coming home late, studying, getting up to go to school, getting on the train again, all those years. It has gotten results. But even if it hadn't, even if I wasn't able to become a champion, I would still know that I gave it my best shot. I tried. I got on the train and tried.[1]

BJORN BORG

Athletes train long and hard day in and day out, rehearsing skills, building strength, and conditioning their bodies. Far too often, however, practice is limited to physical preparation while rehearsal of psychological skills is neglected.

It is an interesting and enigmatic phenomenon. The top athletes and coaches all agree that psychological factors are critical in determining the winner. Sports are said to be largely mental.* An athlete must be "psyched," "mentally tough," and "have his head in the game." Yet, until recently there has been little training and virtually no practice of mental preparation.

For some athletes, this presents no problem. They easily meet the psychological challenges. A little illumination provokes archetypal "Aha"-type experiences and good psychology plugs in easily without any practice. Some athletes, albeit fewer, seem to need no training at all. They seem to be "mentally tough" naturally and meet the challenges seemingly instinctively.

But no matter how well you seem to handle the psychological challenges, most of you do well to recognize that there are improvements to be made. You want to reach greater heights and achieve peak performances more consistently. So it makes sense to give the development of psychological skills some of the

---

*Yogi Berra once said of baseball that "90 percent of the game is mental and the other half is physical."

kind of training, dedication, and discipline you devote to physical training.

I have a friend who owns some undeveloped land just outside of Austin, Texas. Not too long ago, at the end of a day of working and frolicking on his land, he discovered that his gold pocket watch was missing. It must have fallen from his pocket as he romped along the hills. He searched for the watch, retracing his steps from the day as best he could. But it was to no avail. He could not find his watch in the brush and growth of the undeveloped land.

He knew approximately where to look for the watch because he dropped it in an area he traversed often. So he might have chosen to wait in the hope that, in his treks across the land, one day it would jump out at him and be staring him in the face.

But the watch was important to him. It had been a wedding present from his wife and thus had a lot of sentimental value and meaning for him. So the next day he arose bright and early and rented a metal detector. He took this tool and systematically combed his land until he found the watch.

Sooner or later he may have found it anyway. And it would have been nice if he had not had to go to any trouble or expense, but had recovered it serendipitously. But when he did, it might have been the worse for the weather. Or he may never have found it at all! It made much more sense systematically to apply a tool that increased the odds of reaching his goal.

You, too, might fortuitously discover a psychological set that will promote consistent excellence of performance. Acquiring a "mental toughness" with little effort has its appeal. And especially now that you have read this book, you know where to look and might stumble upon good psychology. But I assume how well you perform is important to you! If so, it makes much more sense systematically to practice and employ the tools available for meeting the psychological challenges of sports. You need not wait and hope you will be mentally prepared and mentally tough. You can make it happen. But it takes practice!

Use the psychological tools presented here to rehearse for flawless physical performance. Pay careful attention to the feel of proper execution. Program your muscle memory by repeatedly performing perfectly imaginally.

But don't limit the use of the psychological tools to rehearsing physical practice. Mentally rehearse good psychological performance as well. The physical and psychological are inseparable.

Build scenarios that require successful handling of the psychological as well as the physical challenges. Then imagine yourself in those scenes and practice triumphantly meeting those challenges.

Practice meeting the challenges of motivating yourself to train with consistent intensity. For example, imaginally put yourself in the midst of a hard, boring practice and catch yourself wondering, "Why am I doing this?" or "What am I doing here?" Then plug in your thought control skills and subsequently see yourself producing desired training behaviors and accompanying enjoyment. In this way, practice making even the most grueling and monotonous of practices fun.

Imagine yourself facing a contest that you just cannot seem to get excited about. Then practice getting your head into the game.

Practice turning around those times that you have doubts about doing well. Practice acting confident and feeling confident.

Jack Nicklaus says, "Winning breeds more winning." He suggests, "You learn how to win by winning."[2] Take his advice and imaginally rehearse winning performances again and again.

Pain and fatigue make it difficult to think well and subsequently push on successfully. When you are struggling, your habits take over. Make sure your most practiced responses are ones that accept fatigue, welcome it, and use it as a signal to relax and pour it on.

Picture yourself feeling anxious in the locker room, at the starting blocks, in the batter's box, waiting to receive a kickoff, or the like. Practice coping with the nervousness. Visualize yourself relaxing and turning the anxiety into eager anticipation.

Work on the psychological side of your game consistently and diligently. Jump at every opportunity to rehearse. A combination of physical and psychological practice will yield the highest dividends. Practice plugging in your psychological skills in training and at competitions. And imaginally rehearse a wide variety of situations. The more you invest, the greater your returns.

You may see improvement right away. Or it may take months or even years of practice. But for most people, somewhere along the line something clicks and it all comes together. Then the payoff can be monumental.

Don't get discouraged if it takes a while to realize the benefits of **Championship Sports Psychology**. It may take time for you to integrate the ideas within your personal Challenges and mold the Tools to meet your individual needs.

Stick with it. Tom Fay, editor of *Swimmers* magazine, once suggested, "It's always too soon to quit." He wrote:

> When we have a low day here at *Swimmers*, we remind ourselves of the Chinese Bamboo tree. . . . You plant it, water and fertilize it, and during the first year it doesn't grow. In the second year you water it and fertilize it and it doesn't grow. In the third year you continue to water it and fertilize it and it doesn't grow. In the fourth year, you water it and fertilize it but it still doesn't grow. In the fifth year you water it and fertilize it and it grows—75 feet in six weeks!"[3]

For some of you, the major breakthroughs similarly will come only after persistent action. But with practice they likely will come increasingly more consistently. Then the rewards are tremendous. Winning performances bring about an ecstacy seldom matched. They are worth the practice!

Even if you do not win, if you accept the physical and psychological challenges of sport you will be engaged in your sport in a way that makes your quest for excellence an electrifying and ultimately enjoyable experience. The worst that can happen is something like what former major league pitcher Mike Marshall referred to in describing the duel between pitcher and batter: "I love the individual challenge involved. . . . I love [batters] to challenge me and then, win or lose, I can say, 'Hey, we had a little fun out there.'[4]

Enjoy the challenge!

NOTES

PREFACE

[1]Quoted in KENNY MOORE, "A Night for Stars, Both Born and Reborn," *Sports Illustrated*, Vol. 46, No. 22 (May 23, 1977), p. 34.

[2]PAT HADEN (as told to E. M. Swift), "You Won't Have Me to Sack Anymore," *Sports Illustrated*, September 1, 1982, pp. 152–58.

[3]Ibid.

[4]Quoted in BARRY TARSHIS, *Tennis and the Mind*, New York: Atheneum, 1977, p. 3.

[5]Quoted in MARTY BELL, "The Self-Destruction of Jimmy Connors," *Sport*, Vol. 66, No. 1 (January 1979), p. 55.

[6]SERGE VAITSEKHOVSKY, personal communication, January 6, 1980.

CHAPTER 1:
THOUGHT CONTROL

[1]GARY PLAYER, *Positive Golf*, New York: McGraw-Hill, 1967, p. 23.

[2]TIMOTHY GALLWEY, *The Inner Game of Tennis*, New York: Random House, 1974, p. 20.

[3]Ibid., p. 21.

[4]MAXWELL MALTZ, *Psycho-Cybernetics*, New York: Simon & Schuster, 1960, p. 37.

[5]Quoted in B. J. PHILLIPS, "The Tennis Machine," *Time*, Vol. 115, No. 26 (June 30, 1980), p. 59.

[6]Quoted in JOHN UNDERWOOD, "Open Question," *Sports Illustrated*, Vol. 52, No. 24 (June 9, 1980), p. 82.

[7]Quoted in MURRAY CHASS, "The Case of the Pinstriped Volcano," *Sport*, Vol. 70, No. 5 (May 1980), p. 36.

8Quoted in MARK MERFELD, "Games of the XXI Olympiad, Montreal 1976: Men's Events," *Swimming World*, Vol. 17, No. 9 (September 1976), p. 54.

9Ibid., p. 53.

10Ibid., p. 56.

11In RHODA THOMAS TRIPP, ed., *The International Thesaurus of Quotations*, New York: Thomas Y. Crowell, 1970, p. 297.

12MICHAEL J. MAHONEY, *Cognition and Behavior Modification*, Cambridge, Mass.: Ballinger, 1974, pp. 235–36.

CHAPTER 2:
IMAGINAL PRACTICE

1In RHODA THOMAS TRIPP, ed., *The International Thesaurus of Quotations*, New York: Thomas Y. Crowell, 1970, p. 469.

2LEE PULOS, "Athletes and Self-Hypnosis," in Peter Klavora and Juri V. Daniel, eds., *Coach, Athlete, and the Sport Psychologist*, Champaign, Ill.: Human Kinetics 1979, p. 151.

3JACK NICKLAUS AND KEN BOWDEN, *Golf My Way*, New York: Simon & Schuster, 1974, p. 79.

4BRUCE JENNER AND PHILLIP FINCH, *Decathlon Challenge: Bruce Jenner's Story*, Englewood Cliffs, N.J.: Prentice-Hall, 1977.

CHAPTER 3:
RELAXATION

1Quoted in BOB VERDI, "Athletes Are Pieces of Meat," *Sport*, Vol. 70, No. 5 (May 1980), p. 33.

2JOSEPH WOLPE AND ARNOLD A. LAZARUS, *Behavior Therapy Techniques: A Guide to the Treatment of Neuroses*, New York: Pergamon, 1966, pp. 177–80.

3EDMUND JACOBSON, *You Must Relax*, 5th ed., New York: McGraw-Hill, 1976, p. 203.

CHAPTER 4:
GOAL SETTING

1Quoted in KENNY MOORE, "Give the Girl a Great Big Hand," *Sports Illustrated*, Vol. 51, No. 10 (September 3, 1979), p. 23.

2Quoted in HOWARD SCHNEIDER, "The Private Life of Brendan Foster," *Runner's World*, Vol. 14, No. 1 (January 1979), p. 45.

3Quoted in FRANK BIANCO, "The Iron Tiger," *Sport*, Vol. 69, No. 3 (September 1979), p. 14.

CHAPTER 5:
MOTIVATION

[1]Quoted in RICHARD BENYO, "Walter Stack," Runner's World, Vol. 13, No. 9 (September 1978), p. 72.

[2]Quoted in RICHARD WOODLEY, "The Casual Cruiser," Sport, Vol. 69, No. 5 (November 1979), p. 78.

[3]Quoted in ROBIN FINN, "Brother and Sister—and Best in the World," Sport, Vol. 70, No. 1 (January 1980), p. 64.

[4]Quoted in AMBY BURFOOT, "Craig Virgin: Running in the Fast Lane," Runner's World, Vol. 15, No. 3 (March 1980), p. 56.

[5]Quoted in KENNY MOORE, "Possessed of a Certain Pride," Sports Illustrated, Vol. 56, No. 12, (March 22, 1982), p. 80.

[6]Quoted in BOB OTTUM, "Here It Comes, Special Delivery," Sports Illustrated, Vol. 52, No. 19 (May 5, 1980), p. 36.

CHAPTER 6:
CONFIDENCE

[1]Quoted in BARRY TARSHIS, Tennis and the Mind, New York: Atheneum, 1977, p. 93.

[2]Quoted in FRANK DEFORD, "Still Glittering after All These Years," Sports Illustrated, Vol. 49, No. 26 (December 25, 1978), p. 37.

[3]Quoted in HOWARD SCHNEIDER, "The Private Life of Brendan Foster," Runner's World, Vol. 14, No. 1 (January 1979), p. 46.

[4]Quoted in GEORGE KIMBALL, "The Kansas City Star," Inside Sports, Vol. 2, No. 3 (June 30, 1980), p. 79.

[5]Quoted in KENNY MOORE, "Downhill Racer," Sports Illustrated, Vol. 50, No. 17 (April 23, 1979), p. 29.

[6]Quoted in LAWRENCE LINDERMAN, "The Quiet Steeler, Except on Sundays," Sport, Vol. 70, No. 1 (January 1980), p. 27.

[7]Quoted in BARRY TARSHIS, Tennis and the Mind, New York: Atheneum, 1977, p. 102.

[8]Quoted in DONALD HONIG, Baseball between the Lines, New York: Coward-McCann & Geoghegan, 1976, p. 203.

CHAPTER 7:
PAIN AND FATIGUE

[1]DON SCHOLLANDER and DUKE SAVAGE, Deep Water, New York: Crown, 1971, pp. 14–15.

[2]Quoted in BARRY McDERMOTT, "Supercharger Is Ready to Blast," Sports Illustrated, Vol. 51, No. 8 (August 20, 1978), p. 15.

[3]Quoted in JIM BENAGH, "Thriving and Surviving as an NFL Running Back," *Sport*, Vol. 67, No. 3 (September 1976), p. 41.

[4]Quoted in B. J. PHILLIPS, "The Tennis Machine," *Time*, Vol. 115, No. 26 (June 30, 1980), p. 58.

[5]Quoted in BARRY STAVIO, "Skiing Flat Out," *Sport*, Vol. 69, No. 5 (November 1979), p. 12.

[6]LOTHAR KIPKE, personal communication, January 4, 1980.

CHAPTER 8:
ANXIETY

[1]Quoted in JONATHAN SCHWARTZ, "A Day of Light and Shadows," *Sports Illustrated*, Vol. 50, No. 9 (February 26, 1979), p. 58.

[2]Quoted in "The Kid Is a Contendah," *Sports Illustrated*, Vol. 50, No. 20 (May 14, 1979), p. 71.

[3]Quoted in "Perfect '10,'" *Sport*, Vol. 70, No. 4 (April 1980), p. 81.

[4]Quoted in WM. O. JOHNSON, "The Best at Everything," *Sports Illustrated*, Vol. 42, No. 15 (April 14, 1975), p. 92.

[5]BOB PETIT with BOB WOLFF, *Bob Petit*, Englewood Cliffs, N.J.: Prentice-Hall, 1966, p. 128.

[6]Quoted in DICK CRILEY, "International Gymnast Interview: Kurt Thomas," *International Gymnast*, Vol. 19, No. 9 (September 1977), p. 21.

[7]Quoted in MARK MERFELD, "Games of the XXI Olympiad, Montreal 1976: Diving (Women's Events)," *Swimming World*, Vol. 17, No. 9 (September 1976), p. 76.

[8]Quoted in BARRY TARSHIS, *Tennis and the Mind*, New York: Atheneum, 1977, p. 87.

[9]Quoted in DOUGLAS S. LOONEY, "The Kid's All Heart," *Sports Illustrated*, Vol. 50, No. 10 (March 5, 1979), p. 30.

CONCLUSION

[1]Quoted in B. J. PHILLIPS, "The Tennis Machine," *Time*, Vol. 15, No. 26, (June 30, 1980), p. 59.

[2]Quoted in FRANK DEFORD, "Still Glittering after All These Years," *Sports Illustrated*, Vol. 49, No. 26 (December 25, 1978), p. 37.

[3]TOM FAY, "Looking Back . . . and Looking Ahead," *Swimmers*, Vol. 3, No. 1 (February–March 1980), p. 5.

[4]Quoted in RON FIMRITE, "Mike Marshall, the Best and the Brightest," *Sports Illustrated*, Vol. 51, No. 1 (July 2, 1979), p. 31.

REFERENCES

BANDURA, ALBERT. *Principles of Behavior Modification.* New York: Holt, Rinehart and Winston, 1969.

——————. *Social Learning Theory.* Englewood Cliffs, N.J.: Prentice-Hall, 1977.

BECK, AARON T. *Cognitive Therapy and the Emotional Disorders.* New York: International Universities Press, 1976.

BECK, ROBERT C. *Motivation: Theories and Principles.* Englewood Cliffs, N.J.: Prentice-Hall, 1978.

BELL, KEITH F. "Performance Anxiety." *Coaching: Women's Athletics*, Vol. 5, No. 3 (May–June 1979), pp. 48–49, 82.

——————. "Psychology and Swimming: On Excuses, Rejected Compliments, Public Anger, and Fear of Failure." *Swimmers*, Vol. 3. No. 3 (June–July 1980), pp. 25, 28.

——————. "Psychology and Swimming: Pain Management." *Swimmers*, Vol. 3, No. 2 (April–May 1980), pp. 18–19.

——————. "Relaxation Training for Competitive Swimming." *Swimming Technique*, Vol. 13, No. 2 (Summer 1976), pp. 41–43.

——————. "Self-Instructional Methods." *Swimmers Coach*, Vol. 1, No. 1 (January–February 1979), pp. 29–32.

BELL, KEITH F. and MELVIN R. PATTERSON. "A Self-Monitoring Technique for Enhancement of Swimming Performance." *Swimming Technique*, Vol. 14, No. 4 (Winter 1978), pp. 103–6.

BELL, MARTY. "The Self-Destruction of Jimmy Connors." *Sport*, Vol. 66, No. 1 (January 1979), pp. 48–56.

BENAGH, JIM. "Thriving and Surviving as an NFL Running Back." *Sport*, Vol. 67, No. 3 (September 1976), pp. 32–42.

BENSON, HERBERT. *The Relaxation Response.* New York: Morrow, 1975.

BENYO, RICHARD. "Walter Stack." *Runner's World*, Vol. 13, No. 9 (September 1978), pp. 68–74.

177

BIANCO, FRANK. "The Iron Tiger," *Sport*, Vol. 69, No. 3 (September 1979), p. 14.

BURFOOT, AMBY. "Craig Virgin: Running in the Fast Lane," *Runner's World*, Vol. 15, No. 3 (March 1980), p. 56.

CHASS, MURRAY. "The Case of the Pinstriped Volcano." *Sport*, Vol. 70, No. 5 (May 1980), pp. 34–38.

CRAIGHEAD, W. EDWARD, ALAN E. KAZDIN and MICHAEL J. MAHONEY. *Behavior Modification: Principles, Issues, and Applications.* Boston: Houghton Mifflin, 1976.

CRATTY, BRYANT J. *Psychology in Contemporary Sport.* Englewood Cliffs, N.J.: Prentice-Hall, 1973.

CRILEY, DICK. "International Gymnast Interview: Kurt Thomas." *International Gymnast*, Vol. 19, No. 9 (September 1977), pp. 20–22.

DEFORD, FRANK. "Still Glittering after All These Years." *Sports Illustrated*, Vol. 49, No. 26 (December 25, 1978), pp. 26–37.

ELLIS, ALBERT, and RUSSELL GREIGER. *Handbook of Rational–Emotive Therapy.* New York: Springer, 1977.

FAY, TOM. "Looking Back . . . Looking Ahead." *Swimmers*, Vol. 3, No. 1 (February–March 1980), p. 5.

FIMRITE, RON. "Mike Marshall, the Best and the Brightest." *Sports Illustrated*, Vol. 51, No. 1 (July 2, 1979), pp. 28–36.

FINN, ROBIN. "Brother and Sister—and Best in the World." *Sport*, Vol. 70, No. 1 (January 1980), pp. 60–65.

GALLWEY, TIMOTHY. *The Inner Game of Tennis.* New York: Random House, 1974.

HADEN, PAT (as told to E. M. Swift). "You Won't Have Me to Sack Anymore." *Sports Illustrated*, Vol. 57, No. 10, (September 1, 1982), pp. 152–58.

HONIG, DONALD. *Baseball between the Lines.* New York: Coward-McCann & Geoghegan, 1976.

JACOBSON, EDMUND. *You Must Relax*, 5th ed. New York: McGraw-Hill, 1976.

JENNER, BRUCE and PHILLIP FINCH. *Decathlon Challenge: Bruce Jenner's Story.* Englewood Cliffs, N.J.: Prentice-Hall, 1977.

JOHNSON, WM. O. "The Best at Everything." *Sports Illustrated*, Vol. 42, No. 15 (April 14, 1975), pp. 82–98.

KANFER, FREDERICK H., and JEANNE S. PHILLIPS. *Learning Foundations of Behavior Therapy.* New York: Wiley, 1970.

KIMBALL, GEORGE. "The Kansas City Star." *Inside Sports*, Vol. 2, No. 3 (June 30, 1980), pp. 76–84.

KIPKE, LOTHAR. Personal communication. January 4, 1980.

KLAVORA, PETER, and JURI V. DANIEL, eds. *Coach, Athlete, and the Sport Psychologist.* Champaign, Ill.: Human Kinetics, 1979.

KRUMBOLTZ, JOHN D., and HELEN B. KRUMBOLTZ. *Changing Children's Behavior.* Englewood Cliffs, N.J.: Prentice-Hall, 1972.

LAWTHER, JOHN D. *Sport Psychology*. Englewood Cliffs, N.J.: Prentice-Hall, 1972.

LINDERMAN, LAWRENCE. "The Quiet Steeler, Except on Sundays." *Sport*, Vol. 70, No. 1 (January 1980), pp. 26–35.

LOONEY, DOUGLAS S. "The Kid's All Heart," *Sports Illustrated*, Vol. 50, No. 10 (March 5, 1979), p. 30.

MAHONEY, MICHAEL J. *Cognition and Behavior Modification*. Cambridge, Mass.: Ballinger, 1974.

MALTZ, MAXWELL. *Psycho-Cybernetics*. New York: Simon & Schuster, 1960.

McDERMOTT, BARRY. "Supercharger Is Ready to Blast," *Sports Illustrated*, Vol. 51, No. 8 (August 20, 1978), pp. 14–15.

MEICHENBAUM, DONALD. *Cognitive–Behavior Modification*. New York: Plenum, 1977.

MERFELD, MARK. "Games of the XXI Olympiad, Montreal 1976: Diving (Women's Events)." *Swimming World*, Vol. 17, No. 9 (September 1976), pp. 74–82.

——————. "Games of the XXI Olympiad, Montreal 1976: Men's Events." *Swimming World*, Vol. 17, No. 9 (September 1976), pp. 49–73.

MOORE, KENNY. "A Night for Stars, Both Born and Reborn." *Sports Illustrated*, Vol. 46, No. 22 (May 23, 1977), pp. 32–34.

——————. "Downhill Racer." *Sports Illustrated*, Vol. 50, No. 17 (April 23, 1979), pp. 26–29.

——————. "Give the Girl a Great Big Hand." *Sports Illustrated*, Vol. 51, No. 10 (September 3, 1977), pp. 18–23.

——————. "Possessed of a Certain Pride." *Sports Illustrated*, Vol. 56, No. 12, (March 22, 1982), pp. 68–80.

MURPHY, MICHAEL, and RHEA A. WHITE. *The Psychic Side of Sports*. Reading, Mass.: Addison-Wesley, 1978.

NICKLAUS, JACK, and KEN BOWDEN. *Golf My Way*. New York: Simon & Schuster, 1974.

NIDEFFER, ROBERT M. *The Inner Athlete: Mind Plus Muscle for Winning*. New York: Thomas Y. Crowell, 1976.

OTTUM, BOB. "Here It Comes, Special Delivery." *Sports Illustrated*, Vol. 52, No. 19 (May 5, 1980), pp. 32–37.

——————. "Perfect '10'." *Sport*, Vol. 70, No. 4 (April 1980), pp. 77–81.

PETIT, BOB, with BOB WOLFF. *Bob Petit*. Englewood Cliffs, N.J.: Prentice-Hall, 1966.

PHILLIPS, B. J. "The Tennis Machine." *Time*, Vol. 115, No. 26 (June 30, 1980), pp. 54–59.

PLAYER, GARY. *Positive Golf*. New York: McGraw-Hill, 1967.

PULOS, LEE. "Athletes and Self-Hypnosis." In Peter Klavora and Juri V. Daniel, eds., *Coach, Athlete, and the Sport Psychologist*. Champaign, Ill.: Human Kinetics, 1979.

RIMM, DAVID C. and JOHN C. MASTERS. *Behavior Therapy: Techniques and Empirical Findings*, 2nd ed. New York: Academic Press, 1979.

RUSHALL, BRENT S., and DARYL SIEDENTOP. *The Development and Control of Behavior in Sport and Physical Education*. Philadelphia: Lea and Febiger, 1972.

SCHNEIDER, HOWARD. "The Private Life of Brendan Foster." *Runner's World*, Vol. 14, No. 1 (January 1979), pp. 42–47.

SCHOLLANDER, DON, and DUKE SAVAGE. *Deep Water*. New York: Crown, 1971.

SCHWARTZ, JONATHAN. "A Day of Light and Shadows." *Sports Illustrated*, Vol. 50, No. 9 (February 26, 1979), pp. 56–68.

STAVIO, BARRY. "Skiing Flat Out." *Sport*, Vol. 69, No. 5 (November 1979), p. 12.

SUINN, RICHARD M., ed. *Psychology in Sports: Methods and Applications*. Minneapolis: Burgess, 1980.

TARSHIS, BARRY. *Tennis and the Mind*. New York: Atheneum, 1977.

—————. "The Kid is a Contendah." *Sports Illustrated*, Vol. 50, No. 22 (May 14, 1979), pp. 71–72.

TRIPP, RHODA THOMAS, ed. *The International Thesaurus of Quotations*. New York: Thomas Y. Crowell, 1970.

TUTKO, THOMAS A., and JACK W. RICHARDS. *Psychology of Coaching*. Boston: Allyn and Bacon, 1971.

TUTKO, THOMAS, and UMBERTO TOSI. *Sports Psyching: Playing Your Best Game All of the Time*. Los Angeles: Tarcher, 1976.

UNDERWOOD, JOHN. "Open Question." *Sports Illustrated*, Vol. 52, No. 24 (June 9, 1980), p. 82.

VAITSEKHOVSKY, SERGE. Personal communication. January 6, 1980.

VERDI, BOB. "Athletes Are Pieces of Meat." *Sport*, Vol. 70, No. 5 (May 1980), pp. 25–33.

WOLPE, JOSEPH, and ARNOLD A. LAZARUS. *Behavior Therapy Techniques: A Guide to the Treatment of Neuroses*. New York, Pergamon, 1966.

WOODLEY, RICHARD. "The Casual Cruiser." *Sport*, Vol. 69, No. 5 (November 1979), pp. 76–78.

WOOLFOLK, ROBERT L., and FRANK C. RICHARDSON. *Stress, Sanity, and Survival*. New York: Simon & Schuster, 1978.

INDEX

F

Fatigue, 16, 138–50
    anxiety and, 153
    coping with, 144–46
    countering, 148–49
    cross-country skiing and, 149
    diversions from, 147–48
    excessive tension contributes to, 61,
        142
    fear of, 145
    football and, 140, 145
    imagination and, 147, 150
    muscle, 142, 143, 145
    relaxation and, 146–47
    swimming and, 140, 145
    tennis and, 146
Fay, Tom, 171
Figure skating. *See* Skating
Films, use of, 7, 39, 42, 124, 125
Football
    Brown, Jim, 145
    Campbell, Earl, 105
    confidence and, 126
    fatigue and, 140, 145
    Ham, Jack, 126
    motivation and, 105
    Namath, Joe, 77
    pain and, 140
    Winslow, Kellen, 140
Foster, Brendan, 70, 123
Foster, Robert, 35

G

Gallwey, Timothy, 4, 12, 45
Goals, 64–86
    anxiety and, 158–59
    assessing your, 78–84
    athletic scholarships and, 84
    confidence and, 121
    control over, 82–83
    daily, weekly, and long-term, 70,
        85–86
    definitions of, 64
    determining what direction you
        want to take and, 65–68
    effects of too high a goal, 76
    how high should you set your goals,
        74–76
    limit of, 76–78
    maintaining motivation and, 71,
        110–11
    measurable, 73–74, 79–80
    measuring your progress and, 73–
        74, 79
    perfectionistic, 123
    performance and, 76

Goals (*Cont.*)
    positive, 73
    priorities and, 85–86
    pyramid of, 69–71
    realistic, 79, 158–59
    restructuring of, 83
    satisfaction and, 80–81, 103
    setbacks and, 74
    setting, 64–86
    specific, 72–73
    as standards, 68–69
    success and, 74–76, 121
    swimming and, 70, 74n, 75n, 77, 78,
        80, 85
    time framework for, 71–72
    training and, 105–6, 110–11
    weightlifting and, 76
Goldstein, Stu, 153
Golf
    confidence and, 123
    conscious thought in, 5
    differential relaxation and, 61
    imaginal practice and, 35, 159
    Nicklaus, Jack, 35, 123, 170
    perfection in, 159
    Player, Gary, 5
    videotape used in, 7
Golf My Way, 35
Goodell, Brian, 17
Graef, Jed, 80
Gymnastics
    anxiety and, 161
    Comaneche, Nadia, 158
    differential relaxation and, 61
    imaginal practice and, 46
    perfection in, 158
    Thomas, Kurt, 46, 105, 161
    videotape used in, 7, 39

H

Habits
    bad, 96
    changing, 13–14, 24, 28, 150
    imaginal practice and, 37, 150
    self-motivated training and, 110
Ham, Jack, 126
Heiden, Eric, 95, 105
Hencken, John, 77
Holum, Dianne, 95
Hypoxic training, 70, 82

I

Imagery
    exercises for developing visual, 40
    pleasant scenes, 58

ABOUT THE AUTHOR

Dr. Keith Bell is an internationally known sports psychologist, a champion swimmer, and highly respected coach. He has provided sports psychology services to U.S., Canadian, Australian, and New Zealand National and/or Olympic Teams, has set numerous masters swimming world records, and was selected the United States Masters Swimming 1988 Coach of the Year. Dr. Bell has helped thousands of athletes perform better and enjoy their sport more.

Other Books by Dr. Keith Bell:

- COACHING EXCELLENCE

- PSYCHOLOGY FOR SWIMMERS

- WINNING ISN'T NORMAL

- GOAL SETTING FOR SWIMMERS:
  and other kinds of people.

Did you borrow this book? If so, why not order one for yourself?

——— ORDER FORM ———

Please send to me the following books by Dr. Keith Bell:

___ copies of **CHAMPIONSHIP SPORTS PSYCHOLOGY** . . . . @ $ 21.95

___ copies of **COACHING EXCELLENCE** . . . . @ $ 19.95

___ copies of **TARGET ON GOLD:**
        Goal Setting for Swimmers and Other Kinds of People . . . . . @ $ 8.95

___ copies of The Nuts & Bolts of **PSYCHOLOGY FOR SWIMMERS** . . @ $ 11.95

___ copies of **WINNING ISN'T NORMAL** . . . . @ $ 10.95

___ copies of **YOU ONLY FEEL WET**
        WHEN YOU'RE OUT OF THE WATER:
        Thoughts on Psychology and Competitive Swimming . . . . . . @ $ 16.95

___ copies of **WHAT IT TAKES:** The ABC's of Excelling . . . . @ $ 14.95

___ copies of **WHAT IT TAKES:** The ABC's of Excelling (hardcover) . . . . @ $ 19.95

all prices subject to change without notice

NAME _____

ADDRESS _____

CITY _____ *STATE* _____ *ZIP* _____

Shipping: <u>Surface</u>: Please include $2.50 for the first book ($4.00 for orders outside
the U.S.A.) and $1.00 for each additional book ordered.
<u>Air Mail</u>:   Within the U.S.A. please include $4.00 for the first book and
$1.00 for each additional book ordered. (Outside the U.S.A. include $5.00
for the first book and $2.00 for each additional book ordered.)

Sales Tax: Please add 6.25% sales tax for every book shipped to a Texas address.

Enclosed please find a check or money order for total of $_____ .

For orders outside the U.S.A. please remit an international money order payable in $US.

Please make payable to:

KEEL PUBLICATIONS
P.O. Box 160155
Austin, Texas 78716
(512) 327-1280

Please allow 4-6 weeks for delivery.